Class Act

Changing the Educational Landscape Through *Love*

Christopher Morris

Copyright © 2019 Christopher Morris
All rights reserved. This book or any portion thereof may not be reproduced or used in any manner whatsoever without the express written permission of the publisher except for the use of brief quotations in a book review.

Although the author and publisher have made every effort to ensure that the information in this book was correct at press time, the author and publisher do not assume and hereby disclaim any liability to any party for any loss, damage, or disruption caused by errors or omissions, whether such errors or omissions result from negligence, accident, or any other cause. Views expressed in this publication do not necessarily reflect the views of the publisher. Some names have been changed to protect the identities of the people mentioned.

"Scripture taken from the New King James Version. Copyright © 1982 by Thomas Nelson, Inc. Used by permission. All rights reserved."

Printed in the United States of America

First Printing, 2019

ISBN 978-0-578-56721-1

Christopher Morris Publishing
Chattanooga, TN 37421

Contact Chris

- Book Chris to Speak at Your Event - www.morrisseymodel.com

- Schedule a free call to set up the Morrissey Model Program for my school. - https://www.morrisseymodel.com/book-online

- Follow us on Facebook: facebook.com/morrisseymodel

Contents

Foreword 7

Introduction 9

Chapter 1 Let the Games Begin 11

Chapter 2 Trusting Through the Storm 21

Chapter 3 Time for a Change 27

Chapter 4 A Life-Changing Idea 35

Chapter 5 The First Winners 43

Chapter 6 New Opportunities 51

Chapter 7 A Book and a Plan 59

Chapter 8 Expanding the Vision 67

Chapter 9 Transformed 79

Chapter 10 A Surprising Breakthrough 89

Chapter 11 Making a Difference 97

Chapter 12 The Spiritual War Around You 105

Chapter 13 The Problem Outlined 113

Chapter 14 The System Restructured 121

Chapter 15 The Solution 133

About the Author 141

Foreword

"You have to reach me before you can teach me." It is possibly one of the most widely used clichés in education, but also perhaps the truest. It goes to the core of the idea that you enter the field of education for the kids, not the content. Consequently, many teachers take pride in the efforts they make to connect with their students. They create personal questionnaires for the first day of school. They spend their own money on treats to reward their students. They attend their students' sporting events, concerts, plays, and visit them at work. Surely it is clear that those teachers love their students and are willing to go the extra mile for them. So why would any teacher be interested in this book? Interested in reading more about how love can change their classroom for the better?

Simply put, for many teachers, their idea of showing love to their students isn't working as it should. They still struggle to reach every student. They learn that candy isn't as great an incentive as they thought. Or worse, they realize too late that students take advantage of their kindness. There is a hard truth behind all of this: Loving your students is not the answer if you do not understand how to leverage that relationship to improve both the student and the teacher.

Love, by definition, is a deeply personal connection. Even beyond romantic love, developing relationships only works if two people are committed to each other. Friendships don't form out of generalities. They are bound by a specific connection made between two people. Many teachers lose sight of this when developing relationships with their students. They often make efforts directed toward a whole class, like bringing them food, rather than individualizing their connections. I can't tell you how many times I made this mistake as a teacher. This may come as a surprise to you, but not every child likes candy. So, what happens when a teacher brings bags upon bags of sweets to celebrate an accomplishment? How does that student feel who doesn't eat candy, or can't eat candy? To win the crowd, a teacher may have inadvertently alienated a student. Wouldn't it be better to learn more about what drives each student? What motivates them individually? Imagine the power of personally selected incentives over a pizza party. Imagine what it would mean to that student to know the teacher took the time to remember that specific thing that they love. And now imagine how much harder that student will work once they feel that personal connection.

Showing love for students individually can undoubtedly help, but there is so much more. In this book, Christopher Morris will unlock the crucial pieces you have been missing from your classroom. Learning to care for your students one by one, learning how to develop those relationships, and most importantly, learning how to use those connections to get the most out of each one of your students - and yourself. When you create a sense of personal care, you can use it to create a classroom environment unlike any other. It is not easy work, but who said anything in education was easy? I have had the pleasure of teaching next door to Chris Morris, and I can attest first-hand to the difference he has made in students' lives by showing this sense of personal care. I have also been blessed to watch Chris take this principle beyond his classroom. The journey he is taking to better classrooms across the nation unfolds here in this book, and it is only the beginning. I hope the message rings as true for you as it did for me, and that the results will overflow in your classroom.

Michael Carson
Assistant Principal
Signal Mountain Middle High School

Introduction

When Love came down 2000 years ago, it truly changed it all. It is to this Love, the love of God displayed through the person of Jesus Christ who gave His life for me and my redemption, that I dedicate this story. As you'll find throughout the pages of this book, love changes everything.

It was the fall of 2011. I had just completed a teacher preparatory program in Chattanooga, Tennessee. Seven months earlier, I had married the love of my life after an epic saga only the Lord could have authored.

The school district had recently hired me to teach math in a culturally diverse and impoverished school. A 26-year-old who received a Christian education, I was in for the wakeup call of my life with the realization that not everyone's high school experience is the same. In my case, it wasn't even remotely similar.

For starters, the school to which I was assigned was a Title 1 school. This meant that over 70 percent of the students attending were eligible for free and reduced lunch based on their household income. As mentioned earlier, it was incredibly diverse. The student body was approximately 50 percent white, 34 percent African American, and 16 percent Hispanic or "other."

And then there was Charles. He was a little different from the typical image that you might have in mind when you think of the average American high school student. For starters, he didn't seem overly concerned with what other kids, or anyone for that matter, thought of him. You see, Charles disregarded certain societal norms. He napped during most of my math classes and carried with him a certain air that was unnerving to many. You couldn't help but get the sense that something was off.

It was two weeks into my first year of teaching when the special-education teacher stopped by my room. I remember her rushing through several sheets of paperwork filled with detailed information about how to accommodate students with learning disabilities. And then we came to

Charles. She gave me an entire list of "dos and don'ts" for him, but the only thing I remember was her last three sentences:

"Be careful with Charles. He stabbed his grandfather a few times during the summer with a sword. Yeah, he has homicidal tendencies, but don't worry, he usually does fine at school. Okay, bye!"

"Okay, thanks," I replied. "Wait… Whaaat?!!!"

One might imagine my thoughts and concerns. *What did I get myself into? I'm scared. I'm going to keep my eye on this kid.* I also recalled her mentioning a student that Charles was not to sit next to during class. This kid was in a gang and had a lot of influence over Charles. *Great,* I thought. *He's been sitting next to this gang member for two straight weeks!*

Class began moments later with Charles, the gang member, and a host of other unruly students charging in like a wild stampede. There was one student who randomly barked and made animal noises, then there was Sammy McPherson, who presented his own unique set of challenges.

Sammy self-identified as "white trash" and worked hard at living up to this reputation. In addition to having virtually no attention span, Sammy made a habit of venting out in anger his frustration with me for making him do homework, classwork, or simply any task that he didn't want to do. The best part is they were all in my 3rd-period class. Yes, the animal-noise barker, the self-proclaimed white trash student, the gang member, and—to round the group out nicely—sword-wielding Charles were all stuck with me for an hour and a half each day.

If you've ever worked a sales job where you had to explain to a potential customer why he or she needed your service, then you know there's a lot of effort you must put into it on the front end: identifying the problem, demonstrating that your product will solve it, and convincing the person that it's worth shelling out his or her hard-earned money. This is a daunting task, even if the potential client is interested in the product.

Now, I want you to imagine an even more challenging endeavor. Imagine that you're tasked to force an unwanted product on an audience that is diametrically opposed to receiving it. This is the task of the modern-day teacher — especially teachers who teach high school freshman courses in Title 1 schools.

Chapter 1
Let the Games Begin

"It doesn't matter how stupid, nonsensical, or absurd it appears to you, do what works for your students."
Christopher W. Morris

"Let's begin class by discussing what it means to have a very-uh…"
"Squawk!"
"A very-uh…"
"Woof."
Why is this kid squawking like a bird and barking like a dog? I thought. "A VARIABLE!!!" I shouted in frustration, and I hadn't even finished uttering my first sentence. "No, Charles… put that down! Sammy, why are you out of your seat? Come on, guys."

Many of my classroom disruptions were so off-the-wall, so different from any reaction that one would deem typical or expected, that I would often have difficulty recalibrating. I lost so much class time during those first few months. Between the various characters in my classroom and my inability to get back on track, Lord, help those few kids who were trying to get an education!

On many occasions, I found myself staring off in disbelief, trying to make sense of what was happening, and that was the problem. I was trying to make sense of what I was seeing and experiencing when the simple truth is that there was no making sense of these students' behaviors. What I failed to realize is that they would do anything and everything to keep from doing mathematics. In fact, many considered that they were doing *me* a favor with what they were doing — not improving themselves and thus, not achieving a brighter future. Homework? What's that? I was in the middle of the rudest awakening.

After a couple of weeks of adjusting, wrestling against opposing wills, and asserting my authority, I finally began making some progress, be it ever so little. I would even make it through at least half of the lesson before the period ended. And it was on one of these halfway productive mornings when I experienced my next dose of insanity.

Where's My Red Marker?

"Has anyone seen my red marker?" I naively asked the class. "Seriously guys, where is it?" Irritated and receiving no response, I gave one more look around the room before reluctantly deciding to teach without it.

The day was almost complete–only fifteen minutes left in the period when I noticed something red moving back and forth behind our resident gang member's head. "Is that...?" I asked aloud. I slowly started walking toward the red object moving back and forth when I realized that it was indeed the top to my red marker! As I approached the back of the classroom, the culprit became clear. Charles had my red marker! And he was darkly coloring in something beet red with laser-like focus.

"Charles?" I hesitated. He didn't respond and appeared to be in his own world. "Charles," I said again with a more forceful tone. Still no response. As I got closer, I noticed he was coloring the palm of his hand. Yes, his entire left palm was red, and yet, he continued to color with reckless abandon. "Oh, my goodness..." I spoke softly.

I remembered what the special-ed teacher had said, *He has homicidal tendencies but usually does okay at school.* Why did she say "usually?" "Charles,"

I repeated, nearly begging for a response.

"Mr. Morris?" he finally said.

"Yes."

Charles slowly extended both of his beet-red hands. "Looks like you caught me red-handed," he quipped as he belted a sinister laugh. I don't know if I had ever gone from petrified terror to hilarious delirium in a single instant, but I-burst into laughter and couldn't stop! There were ten minutes left, but I couldn't teach any longer. The entire class and I were laughing – I mean, to the point of tears. This guy was eerily calculated when it came to his humor, and dang it; he got me. He got me good!

That was the end of class for that day. I forgot to assign the homework and once again, completely lost my train of thought, but somehow none of that mattered. I had experienced a breakthrough in my attempt to teach these kids. The breakthrough wasn't another standard mastered or a benchmark reached. It was the beginning stages of forming a relationship. At some level, even though the mysteries of Charles were only beginning to unfold, I caught a glimpse of his personality, his humor – creepy, brilliant, and all!

> The breakthrough wasn't another standard mastered or a benchmark reached. It was the beginning stages of forming a relationship.

It was my first taste of the real secret to teaching: relationship. If I don't know my students, how do I expect to teach them? But I still had so much to learn. I pressed on, ducking and hurdling my way through the bureaucracy of teaching, navigating my way day-by-day. Not only did I have to determine whom to trust and whom not to, but I had to quickly learn the politics of the public school system. Just learning these hidden rules is an education in and of itself. Oh yeah, and then there's teaching. At some point, between keeping one eye on Charles and the gang member and my other eye on all my other responsibilities, I still had to teach math.

And then there are the parents. Anyone who's ever taught a single day knows dealing with parents can be a bigger headache than teaching a problem child. One day, I was trying to facilitate a group discussion between two groups of students. I asked a girl in the class to explain how she arrived at her solution. Her response?

"I already told you, you dummy!"

Once again, the feeling of shock, disorientation, and disrespect overwhelmed my emotions. I could not believe any student could speak to an adult this way. As was policy, I quickly had a short word with the "young lady" and began writing a disciplinary referral to submit to the administration.

I thought my job was complete, and the matter would clearly be deemed the fault of the student, but I was in for yet another surprise. A couple of days later, I received a call from the assistant principal asking me to come to his office. Upon arrival, I was informed that the girl's mother was outraged that she was assigned to in-school suspension, arguing that she had never been in trouble before. I couldn't believe it. Did the mother even know what her daughter said to me? The principal advised me to call the mother and explain what happened to smooth things over. Reluctantly, I agreed and gave her a call.

I just knew that the mother hadn't been told the real story and that, after hearing what her daughter said to me, would take my side. I called her up and immediately suffered the consequences.

"I can't believe you gave my daughter ISS (in-school suspension). Don't you know she's never gotten into any sort of trouble at school?" and on and on she went. I practically had to yell to get a word in. I explained to her the shocking way in which her daughter responded to my simple question.

"Ma'am, your daughter called me a dummy in the middle of class."

"Well," she shot back without skipping a beat, "were you being a dummy?" A fresh wave of shock, disorientation, and disbelief swept over me. Suddenly, I couldn't find the words. I just sat there, mouth agape, bewildered, and angry. This parent didn't have any interest in holding her child accountable but was only concerned with getting her daughter out of trouble, and I was stuck with the problem. You want to talk angry? I was livid!

The math teacher next door was always up for a good "horrible parent" story, so I unloaded. With a lot of guttural laughter and head nodding, she seemed to enjoy knowing that she wasn't the only one dealing with these same kinds of situations.

"Welcome to the club," she exclaimed.

So, this was it. This was the life of a teacher. You just had to bite your tongue, lower your expectations of decent behavior, and take it on the chin from nonsensical parents. I'd like to think that this was the only situation I ever had to deal with, but sadly, that was not the case.

Terrence presented another unique bad student/parent combination. Several times throughout any given class period, Terrence would stand up and start talking loudly to one of his classmates. I could be in the middle of a lecture trying to go through the notes, and Terrence would stand up and start walking around the desks, talking to anyone about anything. That is… anything but algebra.

"Terrence!" I shouted. "Terrence… do you hear me?" He continued talking to Brian about the game last weekend. "Terrence," I said again, "sit down!"

"Why you always picking on me?" Terrence finally responded.

"Ummm. Because you're the only one out of your seat and you're disrupting the class." Blank-faced and aloof, Terrence didn't seem to get the message. Only twenty minutes later, Terrence was once again standing and talking loudly in the middle of the room.

"Terrence!" I said again.

"Why you pickin' on me, Mr. Morris?" By now, I was starting to think I was in the twilight zone. To make matters worse, some of his classmates began to echo Terrence's sentiments. "Yeah Mr. Morris, why you always picking on him?" Were the other kids seeing a completely different scene than I was?

"For one, Terrence, you're standing up. Everyone else is sitting down. For two, you're talking while I'm trying to teach. No one else is. Need I go on?"

This dynamic went on day after day for weeks. I tried talking with him but to no avail. I wrote him up several times, but once again, I found myself in the assistant principal's office over a parental concern.

This time though, things were different. I felt more support from the principal regarding my issues with Terrence. I think he, too, had bumped heads with the young man over the course of the semester. Nevertheless, Terrence's mom was not happy and felt, much like her son, that I was picking on Terrence, claiming that he wasn't having problems with any other teachers. The funny thing was that her claim was a complete "baloney." I had just finished listening to two of Terrence's other teachers complaining to me about the same issues in their classrooms.

"Here's the situation," the principal said. "Terrence's mother is upset and thinks you're out to get her son. I've arranged a three-way meeting between her, you, and me. I'm going to propose that Terrence move to another classroom for the remainder of the year."

It was a great "cover your butt" move on his part. I was not going to argue. I had had it with Terrence, his antics, and his mother. Terrence would inevitably pull the same stunts in his next teacher's class and consequently poke holes in his mother's theory that I was the problem. "Let's do it," I replied.

The meeting took place the next day, and I braced myself for a battle. True to form, the mother implicated that I was guilty several times throughout the meeting. The principal and I held our ground like soldiers in a united front. "My Terrence doesn't come from no broken home," she said emphatically. No one had said anything to her about Terrence's home life, yet she felt compelled to repeat this statement several times.

Unbeknownst to me, Terrence and his brother were known gang members who relied on drug money to support the family. If I had known all of this, perhaps I would've been able to make sense of the situation. The gang mentality isn't about holding each other accountable as much as it is looking out for one another at all costs. You can't "dime" someone else out in the gang, or you could get killed. Nobody cares about right versus wrong. It's about getting each other out of the consequences of their decisions. Gang life is generational. It's no wonder the parents I encountered too often sought only to get their child out of the situation and cared very little about holding them accountable for their actions. It's a totally different mindset.

The conversation went back and forth, but to the assistant principal's credit, he took decisive action. He informed the mother that he would be transferring Terrence to another math teacher's class. I thought this was brilliant. When Terrence would start pulling the same stunts in another teacher's classroom, it would accomplish two things. First, it would absolve any guilt that the mother was trying to assign to me. If the new teacher started having the same complaints about Terrence that I was experiencing, it would be clear where the problem lies. Second, this move would release me from having to deal with him and his mother altogether. I was ecstatic. *See ya, Terrence! See ya, mom! Good riddance,* I thought.

I pressed on and continued to engage in my fair share of parental battles. *How in the world are some of these people allowed to become parents?* I thought on several occasions.

However, Sammy McPherson would perhaps become my biggest test that year. He tried my nerves like no other. It wasn't that Sammy was a bad kid. He wasn't, just utterly annoying. He was always complaining and trying to get out of work. He was hyperactive like you wouldn't believe, continually interrupting my lessons with outbursts of frustration, and to provide some perspective; I wasn't the only one perturbed by his behavior. When he spoke, the girls would roll their eyes in irritation, and many students would make a point to express their own frustrations with his peculiar behavior.

It was a constant tug of war with Sammy that first year. I'd never seen such a lack of discipline in my life. Perhaps no other experience summed up my thoughts on the kid more than one incident that occurred on a spring afternoon. I was trying to answer some emails at my desk in between classes. Charles was already seated with his head on his desk, getting an early start to his usual nap that took place in class. I thought he was asleep, and he probably was, that is, until Sammy pulled one of his trademark tricks.

On the other side of my desk, Sammy was squatting like a baseball catcher. He began popping his head up and down just above my computer screen while shouting, "Can we go outside?" I was trying desperately to ignore him and concentrate on answering my emails, but as usual, Sammy was incessant. He kept bouncing up and down, asking about going outside instead of having class. I held my ground for a few minutes before giving in, acknowledging him for the first time.

I looked up and stared at Sammy in absolute amazement. *How can someone function like this?* I thought. That's when I noticed Charles lifting his head from his nap. From my viewpoint, Charles was positioned perfectly in the background behind Sammy, and once again, Charles' comedic timing got me. He lifted his head while looking directly at me and began circling his index finger around his ear as if to indicate, *he's crazy!* I bellowed in laughter. Here I was, stuck with Charles and Sammy McPherson, and even Charles, with his homicidal tendencies, recognized that "the boy just ain't right." Somehow that helped. Sometimes reality is so crazy that you need to laugh it off. There's no other way to deal with it.

> Sometimes reality is so crazy that you need to laugh it off. There's no other way to deal with it.

I endured various trials that first year. Some days, I felt like I was just scraping by, but I always made it to another day. Sammy was Sammy, and Charles was still Charles, but I finally did have a semi-breakthrough at the end of the year. Providing the material once again was our friend, Mr. Sammy.

It's important to note that in the corner of my classroom was a container with a stack of cardboard pieces. Each cardboard was roughly 15x15 inches. I think another teacher had left them in the room from the year before. I know what you must be thinking. Why hadn't I disposed of them by this point in the year? Frankly, I don't know. They never bothered me and were mostly out of sight. But one afternoon, Sammy decided to put them to use. I had just returned from a trip to the bathroom when I saw Sammy and Ben taking turns slamming their heads into the cardboard pieces trying to break them in half. I think they were attempting to emulate some karate move, but instead of saying "Hi-yah!", they shouted "Aww" each time. As ridiculous as this was, I could tell it was the most fun Sammy had had all week, in or out of school.

"Alright class, it's time to get in your seats."

"Hold on Mr. Morris…Aww," he screamed as he slammed his head into another piece of cardboard that Ben was holding.

"I mean it, Sammy. Have a seat."

"Just a sec… let me do five more," he insisted.

It was then that a thought occurred to me. I've never had any luck whatsoever getting Sammy to do his work. "Hey, Sammy!" I said. "If you can get these ten problems on the board done, I'll let you smash five cardboard pieces." **(LEVERAGE)**

"Really?" asked Sammy. He was so excited. Scratch that. He was absolutely pumped! Sammy immediately ran to his desk and started working out each equation. I've never seen a student work through his assignment so quickly and yet so accurately.

"Okay, Sammy," I said. I picked up a cardboard piece like a karate sensei would hold a wooden plank. Sammy leaned back, excitedly yelled, "Aww," and let go with his best head slam. It was complete satisfaction.

"Let's do it again!" shouted Sammy.

"Okay, but it will require ten more problems." Like a dart, Sammy shot off toward his desk and got to work. We repeated this process for the entire period. Whatever works, I concluded.

Assignment #1:

> ➤ It doesn't matter how stupid, nonsensical, or absurd it appears to you, do what works for your students.

Assignment #2:

> ➤ Once you identify something that your students really want, you can **leverage** it to get them to do what you need them to… even if it's as silly as slamming their heads into cardboard.

Assignment #3:

> ➤ What off-the-wall, silly action can you do to get your students to do their work? It's not about being silly. It's about bending in their direction in order to honor them.

Assignment #4:

> ➤ Don't waste time trying to figure out why your students do some of the things that they do. They'll do anything to get out of work.

Chapter 2
Trusting Through the Storm

*"Peace I leave with you, My peace I give to you;
not as the world gives do I give to you. Let not
your heart be troubled, neither let it be afraid."*
John 14:27

It was the end of year one. I had survived the school year by the skin of my teeth. To my surprise, both Sammy and Charles fared better on the end-of-course examination than I would have predicted. I had concluded that neither one of them was intellectually incompetent but more like socio-emotionally immature. Incredibly immature mind you, but not incompetent. Among the various stunts the two of them pulled was pants-wetting. Oh, have I not mentioned that yet? Yes, this little stunt was a Charles original. In addition to the homicidal tendencies and consistent naps in class, Charles was wetting his pants about once or twice a week at school.

In the middle of any given week, I would see Mrs. Benson, the special-ed teacher, who would alert me to the fact that Charles wouldn't be in 5th period that day.

"Why not?" I always asked.

"Charles wet his pants again. We had to send him home." This was her consistent answer.

Great, I thought. *Just when I was starting to get more comfortable with Charles and beginning to think, 'He's not that strange,' he starts wetting his pants in high school.* This would go on for several weeks in a row before Mrs. Benson and the rest of the faculty would realize the shocking truth.

I was in the middle of teaching my Algebra II class when I heard Mrs. Benson yelling at Charles in the hallway. "Charles, you can't just wet your pants anytime you want to go home!"

"Are you kidding me?" I whispered to myself. Charles had been wetting his pants intentionally this entire time! The more I thought about it, the more it made complete sense. I thought back to when Charles had my red marker the entire class and waited for just the perfect moment to say that I had caught him red-handed. He was calculated. But wetting your pants for the sole purpose of being sent home certainly takes the cake!

Mrs. Benson always made me laugh at key moments. She wouldn't hesitate to let some steam off at students like Charles, but could you blame her? Mrs. Benson quickly took measures to avoid any future pants-wetting issues. Her solution? Backup pants at the school for such occasions. That's right. Several times throughout the rest of that initial year, Charles would change his pants at school from Mrs. Benson's backup supply, so he couldn't use wetting his pants as an excuse to skip class and go home.

You know how most people possess a healthy sense of pride? People generally care what other people think of them, but that was not the case with Charles. Whatever is in your brain that tells you that something may or may not be socially acceptable does not reside in his. Just think about his thought process: "I hate class. I don't want to be here anymore. I know what I'll do. I'll pee in my pants, and that way, they will be forced to send me home!" One thing I'll say about my job, I was never bored. Stressed out? Often. Challenged? Continually. But bored? Never!

Year Two

Remember that deep, ominous tune from the movie, *Jaws?*

"Daaadum...daaadum... daadum dadum dum..." Those two simple notes create a heightened sense of alert, and you know there is going to be

Trusting Through the Storm

trouble. At any moment, a shark will attack its unsuspecting victim. That's a lot like how it feels for a teacher at the end of summer break. That panic you feel when you hear *Jaws* music is the same panic teachers feel when we see the first back-to-school sale commercial on TV. The dread of an imminent attack is at its strongest when we're shopping at Walmart and see backpacks and pencils stocked to the hilt on the shelves. It's inevitable. Our doom is near. It's time to go back to school. It's on to day-long professional development training and updates on the latest policy and curriculum changes. Help!!!

As the new school year began, I was feeling a bit uneasy. I was unsure about how my peers felt about me. At times, I couldn't read people, and it didn't help that I was already insecure about my abilities as a math instructor. I was still new, and not many knew anything about me that didn't pertain to the job. In my mind, the other math teachers couldn't have felt strong about my abilities as a mathematician. I felt like people were always compelled to check on my progress. When the administration would pop into my classroom, it would disrupt me to the point that I had a hard time remembering where I was in the lesson. This would cause me to double-guess my calculations, even if I knew I was doing the math correctly.

It culminated one day when the pressure got to me. I was having a stressful day. The kids were acting crazier than usual, and my classroom management was nonexistent. I fumbled over my words several times. At one point, I realized I was teaching the wrong lesson. Oops! The last thing I needed was another impromptu visit from my principal, but that's exactly what I got. When he walked through the door during my most challenging class, I got startled and jumped with a loud yelp. I explained the equation incorrectly and had to go back and erase my mistake in the middle of class. He gave me another glance as he took some notes and slowly walked toward the marker board. I was so nervous and stressed that when a student raised his hand to ask a question, I didn't notice the laptop power cord wrapped around my leg. With one more step, I launched my school-issued laptop off the podium and on to the floor at my principal's feet. The computer was broken and so was my morale. I dropped my head in absolute failure waiting to be notified that I was fired. It was a fitting end to a horrible day.

The principal didn't say much of anything. He helped me get the busted laptop off the floor and left the classroom. What a way to end the week. That was my last class of the day, and now I had the entire weekend to think about what a miserable failure I had been in front of the principal. I tormented myself with a host of hypotheticals. *What if I get fired? Why would he not fire me? What are my wife and I going to do if that happens?*

I woke up that Sunday morning with fear and anxiety draped over me like a heavy blanket. I felt so low that I had nowhere to look but up. In desperation, I prayed, "Your word says, 'man does not live by bread alone, but with every word that proceeds out of the mouth of the Father!' (Mathew 4:4) Lord, give me a message. Give me a word!"

It was time to go to church. My wife and I left for the service. I was secretly hoping to hear a sermon that was tailor-made for my situation. I remember waiting to hear God say it was time to find a new job, but that was not what happened. The sermon had absolutely nothing to do with my situation at all. In fact, I can't remember one thing about it.

Disappointed, I began to turn down the aisle when I was greeted by a smiling face. A 50-year-old man shook my hand and asked me some general questions about myself. When I mentioned that I was a high school math teacher, his eyes lit up as he shared that his wife was a math major with a heart for education. *Really?* I thought.

"Carolyn… come meet Chris and his wife, Hannah."

In a matter of seconds, I was greeted with the brightest smile I'd ever seen. She asked me about myself, and immediately, I unloaded my work frustrations. When I had finished, she responded with one of my life verses, which I knew was a direct answer to my prayer that morning. She said, "You know, Chris, 'We wrestle not against flesh and blood, but against principalities and powers!'" (Ephesians 6:12). I continually preached this verse to my wife during times of frustration, so when Carolyn quoted it, it had special significance for me. It was a reminder for me that people and circumstances weren't the real problems, but the devil and his demons who work tirelessly against the children of God are the ones pulling strings behind the scenes. They attack us with their weapons of fear and anxiety in hopes that we give up on doing what God calls us to do. Principalities and powers refer to the prince of the power of the air (Satan) and other fallen angels (demons) who although invisible are very real and work to control our thoughts and feelings.

Instantaneously, peace came over me. I realized everything I was struggling with was a tailored attack from Satan and his demons, and I no longer felt fear. Praise God! The shield of faith and the sword of the spirit (the word of God) had won again. At this point in my life, I had learned that God is a God of perfect timing. He knows how to say just the right thing at just the right time to minister to our soul. I knew God had used Carolyn to say precisely what I needed to hear at that moment to release me from the bondage of fear and anxiety and enable me to move forward.

Well, let me tell you just how sovereign and in control God is and what unfolded the very next morning. The principal, to my surprise, had nothing but glowing things to say to me during our post-evaluation conversation. It was customary to have a performance evaluation after every pop-in observation. I was sitting in my evaluation that Monday morning and honestly wasn't sure if he had witnessed what I witnessed the previous Friday at all. I mean… did he even remember me kicking my laptop computer on the floor at his feet and fumbling over my words? He told me how much progress I had made and spoke nothing but encouraging words to me the entire time. *What is going on?* I thought. It was like talking to an entirely different person. I walked out of that meeting in a state of joy and disbelief. I couldn't make sense of it.

God was working, as He always is, behind the scenes ready to prove Himself once my faith was exercised. How much easier would my weekend have been if I had trusted God from the onset instead of wallowing in a state of panic and fear for two days? Lesson learned.

After such a glowing evaluation from my principal, my spirits were restored. But perhaps what encouraged me the most was knowing that God was always there with me, giving me His Word to live on day by day and ever having my back. The job still wasn't easy, but I found the grace to press on toward whatever lies ahead with the confidence that God was with me and had gone before me. Time to man up! I could do this with God's help.

Assignment #1: Remember to laugh

Things to Consider:
- What are some crazy situations that you're in right now that you need to laugh off?
- It will keep you sane.

Assignment #2: God is fighting your battles.

Things to Consider:
- Are there any battles you're facing right now that you need to surrender to Jesus?
- Trusting God can help you avoid stress and maintain your peace.

Assignment #3: God is bigger than your failures.

Things to Consider:
- Don't beat yourself up. God can overcome your weaknesses.
- God has prepared the solution to today's problems before you were created. Don't think of yourself so highly that you feel you're above making mistakes.
- God never created you to live life perfectly. He created you to live life with Him, in relationship.

Chapter 3
Time for a Change

"So then faith comes by hearing, and hearing by the word of God."
Romans 10:17 NKJV

It was the end of year two. Rumors were going around that the district was going to shuffle things up that summer. Translation: there was a strong chance that my principal was going to be moved to a different high school. *"Oh, dear Lord... who will replace him?"* Any teacher knows this can be a stressful ordeal. A principal can mean life or death for teachers in a school. A principal can make life very difficult for you or quite enjoyable and all points in between. Suffice it to say; I was very concerned. I knew two things. I wanted to have a good relationship with my new boss, and I wanted to know who my new boss would be. Would I like this new principal's leadership style? Would he/she like me? My head was swimming with questions, and my heart was pounding in anticipation. After much deliberation, I felt there was a good chance that the assistant principal of our high school would be promoted to his position as principal.

I waited a few days before finally hearing my suspicion confirmed that she would be the new principal. Praise the Lord! This was huge for me. I already had a good relationship with my assistant principal, who was now in charge. It was a breath of fresh air. I now had an ally. The year before, my new boss had already proven to me that she had my back.

I had been having issues with a student who was behaving like a brat. There was no other way to describe it. Her behavior was so outlandish that she saw nothing wrong with standing up in the middle of a test and asking the other boys in class to look at her pants to see if she had a stain on them. Not only did she talk during a test, but she distracted all her classmates, especially the boys. She was a flirt and used to getting what she wanted. Let's just say; I don't think she was concerned if there was a stain on her clothes. Believe me! None of the boys in that class were looking for stains if you know what I mean. I told her at that moment, and at many other moments in that class, to please stop talking/distracting her classmates, but she would always respond the same way: "You don't have to be rude about it!" This was her way of disorienting you so that she would get her way.

"Sherry, please have a seat and stop talking during the test!" I'd say, repeatedly.

"Well, you don't have to be rude about it!" she'd reply.

Well, apparently, I do have to be rude about it because nothing else is getting through that thick head of yours, I would think.

It was not a good situation. I needed to get the administration involved. After considering the dynamics and thinking things through, I came to the following conclusion. I needed a female's backing and support with this situation. The reason was simple. This Sherry girl had a way with men. She wasn't bad-looking and, as I described earlier, was very flirtatious. I needed support from someone immune to her charms.

For this reason, I sought support from the only female administrator in our building. Man, was that a great call! She was awesome.

Sherry tried her best to justify her behavior to the assistant principal. She listed off my faults, as she saw them. "He's sarcastic!" she told her. "He's this... and that..." Sherry added. The principal wasn't having any of it. Booyah!

"I don't want to hear another word of you talking back to Mr. Morris or pulling more of these stunts," she told Sherry.

"Let me move to a different classroom," Sherry responded.

"You don't get to make those kinds of decisions," said the assistant principal. "From now on, you are not to say a word to Mr. Morris when he tells you to do something. If you have to stay quiet throughout the whole class, then that's what you'll have to do."

Sherry started tearing up like a petulant child who isn't getting her way, trying to cry until she gets what she wants. Again, the assistant principal wasn't buying it.

From that moment on, I felt a sense of support from and goodwill toward her. When I had an issue, I went to her. I was elated that my former assistant principal was to become my new boss.

My sentiments were never more validated than at the end of the school year during our annual end-of-the-year faculty roast hosted by Mr. Dunshire, one of the school's English teachers. He had an absolute gift. I'm convinced he could host a Tonight Show on a major network if he wanted to. He had a way of making fun of just about everyone at work without offending them. Well… maybe he offended a few people, but nothing too bad. It was a great way to let the steam off after all the ridiculous things that took place throughout the school year.

He held nothing back and even took a shot at our new boss and principal with one of his jokes. Everybody gasped and held their breath. He was roasting our new boss! If you knew the people involved, it would have had you rolling in with laughter with that sense of, "I can't believe he just said that!" He could poke fun of the new boss to her face, and let me tell you … he did, and she laughed more than anyone else in the room. It would be well received. I wish I possessed that talent, but alas, we all have our limitations. It showed a lighter side to her personality. She could laugh at herself and not take things too seriously. In my eyes, this is an admirable quality.

I only felt that sense of being stressed when someone from central office popped into my room from time to time. On the few occasions when someone from the central office would visit me, my stress would kick in full gear. Looking back, perhaps I did need accountability. With my new-found freedom came a few bad habits. One habit was my tendency towards laziness. The district had selected an excellent textbook company that included a database of PowerPoint lessons that perfectly matched to each unit in the curriculum. You could literally click through the lesson's PowerPoint every day, and it would do all the work for you. Instead of switching things up, incorporating illustrations or group activities, I fell into the trap of clicking through that PowerPoint on far too many occasions.

The kids were bored. I was disenchanted. And things all came to a head one afternoon when central office personnel decided to pay an impromptu visit to my classroom. They were all there, staring and glaring at every move I made. I was lecturing, which I knew they did not like, but I had the kids' attention. Once again, I refused to put on a show just because a few visitors stopped by for ten minutes. They wanted to see me asking specific questions designed to elicit student engagement, as outlined in the county "best practices" booklet. Honestly, I simply didn't believe any of that stuff worked. It just wasn't practical. At the end of the day, when I was speaking with my department head, I was informed by her that the central office observers were not satisfied by what they had seen in my classroom and felt that I was digressing. *Ugghh!!!* I was upset. They went for months without seeing you and then they would just pop into your room for ten minutes and make snap judgments. "I'm over it!" I said.

I left work that day feeling burned out and hopeless. "They just want me to be their puppet while they play puppet master!" I told one of my best friends, Daryl, on the phone. He and I had met when we were working for an insurance company in town. Even though he was old enough to be my dad, we had the sort of friendship that trumped the generational gap. He was a strong Christian who always pointed me to Christ and challenged me to take a literal interpretation of Jesus' teachings in the Bible. "Just trust God," he would always say. My relationship with him helped to guide me through trying times leading up to my marriage to my wife, Hannah. He would often remind me that the Christian life is simple. It all comes down to obedience and trusting what God is telling you to do. Jesus always told others that He only did the will of His Father. He only said what the Father told Him to say and did what the Father told Him to do.

Daryl lived in Texas at the time but was in town visiting. We agreed to go out to dinner to catch up and discuss my frustrations. At a local Japanese restaurant, I began to unload on him what was bothering me. "They don't care what I think or even what makes sense! The powers that be want me to play their game at all costs. It's so controlled," I said. Throughout my venting spells, Daryl would remind me that God put me there for a reason.

"Why don't you come up with your own approach?" he said.

"Yeah…right," I replied. Daryl insisted.

"Go up to the administration and say, hey, give me one year. I'm going to try it this way. If things don't improve you can make me go back to the old way," he suggested.

"You're full of it," I responded. "There's no way they'll go for that."

About that time, as the waitress was dropping off our checks, the spirit of the Lord spoke to me as clearly as ever. Immediately, I heard, "Your skills will accomplish what the force of many cannot." The words pierced my spirit, and I knew they were truth. "For the word of God *is* living and powerful, and sharper than any two-edged sword, piercing even to the division of soul and spirit, and of joints and marrow, and is a discerner of the thoughts and intents of the heart." (Hebrews 4:12) At that single moment, I knew that I was completely wrong and experienced absolute humility. I mean, I thought Daryl was full of it. Before God spoke to me, I thought there was no way Daryl was right about this one. I was convinced. But with just a few choice words, the Lord had convinced me otherwise. I told Daryl what the Lord had just spoken to me. His grin went from ear to ear as he burst into laughter. He had one of those infectious laughs that everyone loves, but, at the moment, I couldn't appreciate it!

> "Your skills will accomplish what the force of many cannot."

We both knew God was going to do something with me at that school that only He could do, but we had no idea what. "Well, it's not math!" I told Daryl. I barely felt competent in algebra and as far as geometry went… forget it. It's a strange feeling knowing something about your future is a certainty yet not knowing how it's going to happen or what it will look like. But that's where I was. A night or so later while I was drifting off to sleep, I noticed another God clarifier. It has long been my custom to listen to Focus on the Family's long-running audio series called *Adventures in Odyssey*. My sister was obsessed with it as a child, and it eventually rubbed off on me. I was listening to an episode on my headphones while going to sleep and couldn't help but notice that the theme of the episode was eerily familiar to my situation.

> It's a strange feeling knowing something about your future is a certainty yet not knowing how it's going to happen or what it will look like.

In the episode, Connie, the Sunday School teacher, was getting complaints from her kids about her classes. They said that her lessons were boring and that's why so many of them stopped coming to her classes. At the end of the episode, Connie realized that she had been lazy when it came to planning her Sunday School lessons, and the kids noticed. They responded in kind, and it was causing things to go poorly for her class. At the end of the episode, Connie realized that she was the problem and repented of her slack approach in her role as a Sunday School teacher. I was completely convicted. I knew that God was using this episode to call me out on my laziness on the job and reveal why things had turned out the way they did at work. It was time to repent.

I knew God was nudging me for my laziness with lesson planning. He had made it very clear. His words were, "Your skills will accomplish what the force of many cannot." What skills? Again, I believed, but I had no clue what He was talking about. The only thing I knew to do was put more effort into my lesson planning. I decided, out of an attempt to obey, that I would spend a minimum of an hour and a half for every lesson for two weeks. I followed through and put in the work. I made sure to work through every problem and anticipate how my students would try to solve them. After a week or so of this discipline, I noticed a difference taking place. I began to access a level of creativity that I never knew I had. Ideas would come to mind during my planning that never occurred to me before. I would think of adding a picture, video, or game in my lessons to make them both fun and appealing. The funny thing was that I was starting to have a little fun too. And it was during one of those long lesson planning sessions that I stumbled upon the best idea of my educational career.

Assignment #1: Invest yourself in your work.

Things to Consider:
- Put in the time.
- Creativity is born out of your work.
- Are you putting in the work?
- You're more creative than you think.

Assignment #2: You can choose!

Things to Consider:
- You can choose your attitude, whether good or bad.
- Your students will respond to you in kind.
- Choose a good one!

Assignment #3: Choose to be excellent.

Things to Consider:
- Are there areas in your life where you need to put forth more effort in a spirit to be excellent?
- For me, it was committing to at least an hour and a half of lesson prep time.
- What would this look like for you?

Chapter 4
A Life-Changing Idea

*"In life, we never get what we deserve but what we
have the leverage to negotiate."*
Jalen Rose

    While at home, I was thinking through my lesson for the next day while watching television. During one of the commercial breaks, a preview for the Academy Awards aired on the screen. Being a typical guy, I was flipping between three or four channels. I switched over to ESPN and saw they were airing a commercial for their upcoming ESPY Awards show. I started thinking. *What is it with these awards shows? They have this sort of universal appeal. Folks either want to win or be nominated, and the rest of us can't wait to see who wins. It holds everyone's attention.* Not only this, but people seem to be very motivated to work their tails off to win these awards.

    It seems to work in Hollywood as well, with the Academy Awards. It works in the music industry with the Grammys. Now the athletes are getting in on the action with the ESPY Awards. *Why wouldn't this work in education?* I started thinking. *How would this look in the classroom? It needs to be our own thing, something my classes will take ownership over.* Then I thought, *I want to give my students an award named after me.* I wanted to use it to motivate the kids to put forth the necessary effort to have success academically. I knew

I didn't want the kids to win the award based on academic achievement. I decided I'd have the students win the award based on improvements in their character and habits. *That should work,* I thought. *Now I just need a name. What should I call it?* I called for my wife. "Hey, babe. I want to do an awards ceremony for students based on their improved efforts in their character. What do you think of the Morriscars?" She gave me a look that could send chills up your spine. "Okay...okay..." I said. After a brief pause, I said, "I know. What about the Morrissey Awards? We could call them the Math Morrissey Awards." She smiled and gave me a "thumbs up." We had a winner.

I knew I wanted the awards themselves to be certificates with my brand name on them. Each award certificate would explicitly say what each kid did the previous week that showed growth in character. I would include inside jokes and any pictures that went along with the theme of that award. If a student won an award for staying awake throughout class when they would typically take a nap, I would include a picture of an alarm clock sounding with a tag that said something like "rise and shine." I had no graphic design experience or skills. I started by opening a Word document and creating them on that. Without much more of a plan than this, I decided I was going to pitch my idea to my students the following Monday.

Midway through my first class on Monday morning, I surprised my students by playing an impromptu musical number. I had pulled up a YouTube video that played Oscar-style background music and blared the volume to the max. A few seconds into the song, I started my pitch. "From now on, every Monday for the rest of the school year, we will be holding what I'm dubbing the Math Morrissey Awards ceremony. Morrissey Awards have nothing to do with math. Morrissey Awards are about your character. How do I win a Morrissey Award? You may ask. I will give you some examples. Darren, do you think you could take just one or two naps next week instead of your usual five? Susan, how about you go an entire class without gossiping about another girl that you don't like? Timmy, how about you turn in the assignment I've been asking you to turn in for three weeks now? Watch out... the eyes of Morrissey are looking at you!"

To be honest, I had no idea how the students would respond. My gut said that a lot of the kids would act like they were too cool to show that they care, but I knew, secretly, a few of the kids would want to win. To my surprise, the kids loved it and didn't hold back. Out of thirty total students, twenty-two of them stood to their feet with applause shouting with excitement. "You're going to win teacher of the year with this!" yelled one of the boys. *Are you serious?* I thought. "I mean... yeah!" I quickly got into character. Their response is what sticks with me the most. I repeated the same pitch to every class that day and got similar reactions. *This is hilarious,* I thought. I hadn't even given out an award yet. All I had done was sell the concept and create a deep desire for personal acknowledgment in front of their peers. Here's a heads up for those who didn't catch it. Personal acknowledgment in front of their peers is the number one thing school-aged students want more than anything else.

> Personal acknowledgment in front of their peers is the number one thing school-aged students want more than anything else.

But it was so much deeper than that. I was offering the students a chance to become a better version of themselves. The idea was to recognize where the students were and who they were and call them just a little bit higher. I wanted to ignite a desire for self-improvement one step at a time. Monday was a success, but the kids' responses were nothing compared to what transpired the rest of the week. The very next day was telling. At my school, we had five minutes between classes for students to get to their next period. It was my only window to unwind, go to the restroom, and chat with colleagues. After first period, as I was walking down the hall, I felt a tap on the shoulder from behind. It was Brittany from third period. With a whisper and a real effort to be discreet, she leaned into my ear and asked me a question. "Mr. Morris," she said. "I really want a Morrissey. What do I have to do to get one?" *Oh my gosh,* I thought. Having completely forgotten about the awards, I quickly recalled the previous day's events and realized something. These kids really want these things. **(LEVERAGE)** "Hey, Brittany," I said. "I don't want to see or hear you talking junk about Sarah behind her back anymore this week."

"Done!" she replied. She then walked off without another word. *No negotiation?* I thought. *No talking back? That's different... and amazing!!!*

A couple of minutes later, I felt another tap from behind. It was Joe from fifth period.

"Yo, Mr. Morris, what I got to do to get a Morrissey, dog?" Joe asked.

"How about you turn in last week's homework by this Friday like I've been asking you all week?" I said.

"I'll have it turned in tomorrow," he replied. **(GOING ABOVE AND BEYOND)**

Again, like Brittany, Joe darted off without another word. The crazy thing was that Joe's homework was in the box before I even got to work the next morning, and the assignment was done to completion. Some of the answers were even correct! That had never happened before. Even better! That kind of interaction between my students and me occurred more than ten times that day.

> It was like, for the first time in their lives, they had a reason to play this game we called school.

Every student thought he or she was the only one to have this sort of "inside deal" with me, and I just let them believe that. It was incredible! The best part was that every student who asked me what they needed to do to earn an award **changed their behavior immediately**. It was like, for the first time in their lives, they had a reason to play this game we called school.

I was starting to suspect that maybe this Morrissey idea was what God was talking about when He said, "Your skills will accomplish what the force of many cannot." Any doubts were all but laid to rest when Thursday rolled around. It was the end of the day. I was attempting to teach the hardest lesson I was tasked to teach that year: inverse logarithmic functions. Most of you reading this book probably have no idea what I just said. Neither did any of my students. Fifteen minutes into the lesson, the students were looking at me like I was speaking Chinese. It was at this time that I got interrupted by one of the most challenging students I taught that year: Eddie. Eddie was a known Crip gang member. I had to have monthly meetings with the assistant principal and school resource officer, so I knew what to look for in my classroom. There were gang signs I had to look out for. I wasn't allowed to let Eddie wear anything blue, and if I noticed that he was, I was to notify the SRO or assistant principal immediately.

You see, Eddie was moving up in the gang world. He was brilliant intellectually. He wasn't dumb enough to be doing the drive-by shootings, but he was probably orchestrating them. There was a situation going on at the time that was especially sensitive. Police officers were investigating whether Eddie's gang was trying to organize a hit on another student in my first block class by shooting up his house. Unbelievable, I know, but somehow, I was supposed to keep an eye on all that while, at the same time, finding time to teach a little algebra.

Anyway, now that you have the backstory let's go back to my lesson on inverse logarithmic functions. I was staring at a bunch of blank faces when Eddie started walking towards me in the middle of class. Before I knew it, he had snatched the marker out of my hand and began working the problem on the board while shouting at his classmates, "Look, y'all, it's not that hard!" To my surprise, Eddie began working out the problems to perfection, explaining his steps along the way. The other kids started asking him questions and, amazingly, he answered every single one. I finally just sat back and watched the whole thing transpire with my mouth agape in disbelief. I knew he was smart, but he was always too cool for school, literally. Every attempt I had previously made to teach him failed as he seemed more interested in protecting his "gangsta" reputation.

But not today! He was a rock star! I let him teach on for nearly twenty minutes before he handed the marker to me and took a seat. "That was perfectly correct, Eddie. Does anyone have any other questions?" I asked. After shaking off my amazement, I proceeded with the day's lesson and resumed teaching. About fifteen minutes more into the lesson, I noticed Eddie's hand raised in the back of the class.

"Yes, Eddie?" I said. "What's your question?"

"Mr. Morris, I need to talk to you," he said.

"I'll have a minute after class if you want to stay after," I replied.

"No, Mr. Morris, I need to ask you something right now. Can you come over here?" he insisted.

Hesitantly, I started walking toward him, hoping he wasn't going to pull some crap. I think the entire time that I was walking his direction, I was silently praying to Jesus for His protection. I leaned over with my ear toward him, and he whispered something that caught me completely off guard. "Look, man, what I got to do to get a Morrissey?" He gave me a gesture that implied that everything he did that day on the board was in hopes to earn an award. "Holy Crap!" I said out loud.

> This kind of personal recognition so deeply connects with students that it has the power to draw young people away from gang activity and back toward their education.

Oooohhhhh!!! I think I'm seeing what God was talking about now. Yep. Okay, here we go. This is huge! I thought. This kind of personal recognition so resonates with students that it has the power to draw young people away from gang activity and back toward their education. Think about that. It could heal a nation. I literally couldn't wrap my mind around how impactful this could be.

It's imperative to keep in mind that all of this transpired the very first week that I unveiled the idea. I hadn't even given out an award yet! Honestly, I wasn't even sure what the award was going to look like. That weekend, not knowing how else to go about it, I opened a Word document and started playing around with ideas. I finally settled on Algerian font, enlarged the font size, and branded the award the Math Morrissey Award. I taught four classes that year, so I decided I was going to make at least one award for each one of the classes. In that way, every student got the sense that they could be the winner each week. I may have made two awards per class that initial week. I kept the design simple. I would create a unique theme for each one based on the breakthrough I noticed from the winning student that week. For example, if Johnny from first period exhibited noticeable self-control during class instead of blurting out whenever he felt like it, he might win the "Self-Control" Morrissey Award for Outstanding Display of Composure. At the bottom of the certificate, I would write a paragraph-long description of what Johnny did that was different from his usual pattern of behavior. This section would be extremely personal like I was writing him a short letter. I would lightly touch on how he used to behave, but then spend most of my words highlighting and encouraging what he specifically did right the previous week. If possible, I'd find a funny picture on Google that showed someone displaying self-control and paste it on the award.

The funny thing was that just taking the time to sit down and make these awards put me in a better mood. I started becoming mindful of the unique qualities of my students and appreciating them more. Any clever things that came to mind while making the awards, I'd be sure to include on the award. If there were any inside jokes that I knew the whole class would appreciate, I would reference them on the award for that student. In this way, the awards were fun for everyone in the room, not just the recipient of the award.

Assignment #1: Offer value to your students

Things to Consider:
- ➢ Are you offering something to your students that they truly value?
- ➢ Do you find that they're willing to work harder to attain what you're offering?
- ➢ If you want to get better results, you must have something of value in the eyes of your students. Once you have something of value from their perspective, you can offer it in exchange for their effort.

Assignment #2: Find a way to gain leverage

Things to Consider:
- ➢ The degree to which students value your offering will be the degree that they are willing to change.
- ➢ This is the essence of LEVERAGE!
- ➢ Remember… you get out of life what you have the LEVERAGE to negotiate!

Chapter 5
The First Winners

"Talk is cheap, actions are expensive. Don't talk about it until you're able to afford the action."
Bar Refaeli

I remember one of the first students who won my Morrissey Award. She was an excellent student. She didn't just complete her assignments on time. She was thorough, mindful, and carried with her a maturity that was beyond her years. I often got the sense that she felt like the adult in the room compared to her peers, maybe even, at times, compared to me. She had so much potential with a real shot at going anywhere and doing whatever she wanted to do in life. Yes, she had a lot of upside and yet I felt that there was just one thing holding her back from all that potential. You see, she was a complainer. Not just a few grumbles here or there. It was incessant!

Unlike her peers, she would always comply with my directions. She would do what I asked of her in the end. But not without first providing a few remarks, groans, and sarcastic comments. For months, I put up with them because, after all, she was doing what I asked her to do. Many of the other students in the class wouldn't comply at all. But eventually, I came to realize that I should expect more from her because she deserved it.

I decided that I would award this young lady if and only if she took me up on my impending challenge. One day I looked her in the eye and said, "I want to see if you can go an entire class without uttering one complaint." Her expression was priceless with a mixture of shock and bewilderment. "Why would I do that?" she replied. "That's ridiculous." Not knowing what to do with me, she shook her head, visibly confused, and headed for her desk. The next day before class she stopped me in the hall and said, "I talked to my mother about what you said… she told me I don't have to do what you asked me to do yesterday." After a brief pause, I replied, "I know you don't have to do what I asked, but you could choose to do it." I wish I could describe the look on her face after my response. It was entertaining, to say the least. "Ughh! I'm going back to my seat," she said and stomped off.

That was the end of this exchange. I thought nothing of it for a couple of days until one morning, when I had been teaching for nearly an hour, she spoke up in class with a question.

"Mr. Morris!"

"Yes…?" I looked at her, expectantly.

"Did you notice?" she asked.

"Notice what?" I responded.

"I haven't complained at all today," she said proudly.

Really? I thought.

After consideration, I realized not only had she not complained for sixty minutes into the lesson, she hadn't said anything at all. I nodded. With a smirk, she glanced my way as if to say, "Game on!" Sure enough, she lasted the entire period without one single complaint, or hardly one word for that matter.

"I have to say; I'm proud of you. I didn't think you could or would do it."

"Mr. Morris", she replied. "I didn't complain even one time… but I thought a lot of thoughts!"

Even I couldn't help but appreciate the inherent sass and wit she possessed. But I tell you what. Though she still complained periodically throughout the rest of the year, it was never as prevalent. As I intended, she won the "No Whiny" award the following week for lasting an entire period without a single complaint and she took ownership over it. I included a picture of her favorite singer, Justin Bieber, with a caption that said, "a free Bieber song in class this week". Everybody knew she was obsessed with Justin Bieber, so I decided to have fun with it. I told her that she got to choose when she wanted the Bieber song to be played. She only had one opportunity, but whenever she gave the word, I had to stop what I was doing and play a Bieber song.

> She loved it not only because she was being honored, but because she was being afforded a small bit of power for that week.

It went well. She loved it not only because she was being honored, but because she was being afforded a small bit of power for that week. And when I followed through on the terms of our deal and stopped teaching to play a Bieber song, it showed the rest of the class that my words carried weight and that it could happen for them, too!

The process had applications for almost any dynamic or behavior patterns I wanted to correct. Perhaps one of the most telling examples of the power of this process occurred a week later. There was a girl in the same class with a learning disability. I think she was mildly autistic. It was subtle enough that, even though teachers knew something was a little bit off, the other students didn't always pick up on it. In addition to Kianna's learning disabilities, she was steadily becoming the class punching bag. The problem was that Kianna brought it on herself. She would say offensive or insensitive things to her classmates periodically, which only helped to foster a "gang up on Kianna" climate in the room. I wanted to change this. But how? After consideration, I decided to take a tactical approach and call in some recruits for my mission.

"Kate, Ashley, come over here for a second. I need your help," I said, one day when I had had enough.

"What is it, Mr. Morris?" they replied.

"You know Kianna from class?" I asked.

With noticeably annoyed expressions and their eyes rolling, they responded. "Yes... why do you ask?"

"The next time Kianna says something that ticks you off, I want the both of you to say something nice to her." There. I had thrown down the gauntlet.

They were shocked. "What? That's crazy. Why would you ask us to do that?"

"Well, I have a lot of respect for you guys and want you to lead in this area for me. Just try it."

"I don't know. Mr. Morris…" They were both skeptical.

"Try!" I insisted.

"…Okay…" They agreed, somewhat reluctantly.

As though waiting for her cue, Kianna walked around the corner toward the classroom and shoved Kate and Ashley, shouting… "Out of my way!"

"Now's your opportunity, girls! Go for it!" I reminded them.

"Kianna… We like your hair." Good first try.

I looked at the girls as if to suggest that they could do better.

"Kianna, we like your shoes."

"Kate… Ashley… can't you say something nice to Kianna about her as a person?" I offered.

"Nope, that's as good as we got, Mr. Morris." They had a point, I guess.

"Fair enough." I agreed.

I began teaching and had nearly forgotten about the incident when I noticed the start of an interesting dynamic. Every fifteen minutes or so, when Kianna would make her usual snappy and irritating comments to her classmates, Kate and Ashley would yell, "Kianna, we like your sweater!" Another time the girls yelled, "Kianna, we like your scarf!" Even though Kate and Ashley were having fun with this, it always caught Kianna off-guard. "…Thank you," she would respond hesitantly. Eventually, Kianna seemed to lose some of her bite, and a healthier, safer classroom environment grew throughout the week. The dynamic culminated at the end of the week when Kate offered to get Kianna a damp rag when Kianna was suffering from an upset stomach. Kate even began to rub Kianna's back until she felt better. Perhaps the most fantastic element of Kate, Ashley, and Kianna's story took place after Kate's award. Two months later, it became clear to me that a real change had taken place in the hearts of both Kate and Ashley.

I walked into the lunchroom and noticed Kianna sitting with Kate and Ashley at the lunch table. Kianna used to always sit by herself with only her comic books to keep her company.

"Why, what is this? How long has this been going on?" I inquired.

"We have been letting Kianna sit with us every day, Mr. Morris! Kianna is still snarky toward us, but we make sure she sits with us every day." Kate and Ashley had not told me about this before. I was dumbfounded. I couldn't believe they were behaving this way for months and didn't even feel the need to let me know about it. They had simply experienced a change of heart towards Kianna and genuinely decided to look after her. Wow, God!

> This process intrinsically shaped character and behavior in a way that was permanent.

This was a game-changer! It was so entirely different from the Pavlovian processes so prevalent in education today. It wasn't a point system or a series of stickers one earned to comply with the wishes of the authority figure. This process intrinsically shaped character and behavior in a way that was permanent. If a student wins a caring award, he begins to see himself as caring. He wants to live up to his new identity and, therefore, continues in the awarded behavior long after he wins. In fact, he eventually stops caring about the incentive altogether. Huge!

Many amazing transformations like these took place in those three months. I was continually blown away! It was so evident that God was doing something new and revolutionary through me and this process. Just in case I needed any more evidence, toward the end of the semester, God sealed His case! The entire dynamic of my classes had changed. Kids were excited to come to math class. Let me say that again. Kids were excited to go to MATH CLASS! It was fun! I know this because the students were telling me so. The Morrissey Awards were motivating for the kids and made them want to work harder than usual. I became very mindful of my students and made sure to mix things up, add humor, and look for ways to present the content in more engaging ways. Everyone was having fun, including me!

A "know, like, and trust" dynamic was cultivated between my students and me, and it made all the difference. With just a couple of weeks left in the school year, God opened the door for something heavenly. We had just finished the annual End of Course examinations. The school year was pretty much over. Most of the teachers were playing educational games and waiting out the clock until the last day of school. I had promised my students that if they worked hard and studied diligently, we'd have a party after the standardized examinations. During the party, we'd eat food, watch a clean movie, and hang out. About forty minutes into the class, I overheard an interesting argument among three of the girls in the class. To my surprise, it was an argument about Jesus. Monica, a bright young lady, and leader in that class expressed her doubts as to how Jesus could have gone forty days and forty nights without food or drink. "It's just not possible," Monica said. One of the girls yelled back, "Jesus was God so He could do anything." It was at this moment that I felt compelled to interject.

"Actually girls, Jesus did last forty days without food or drink, but it wasn't because of His deity," I said. "Jesus was fully God and fully man, but he chose to limit Himself and only live out His life in His humanity as an example for us to follow. "Then how did He last forty days without food?" Monica quickly questioned. Before I could get any response, I believe the Holy Spirit answered her question directly. "Oh, God gave Him the strength?" Monica said, answering her own question. "Exactly!' I said.

> All we need to do is speak the truth. There's no need to defend it.

In the New Testament, Jesus frequently told believers that they were blessed because the Lord Himself revealed certain truths to them. He pinpointed the source of their specific understanding. Most of the time, it was when a believer confessed to Jesus that He was the Christ. Jesus would reply that God had revealed this to them.

In this instant, I believe the Holy Spirit revealed to Monica the truth of this story. It was as if it just hit her like a ton of bricks. "Oh, God gave Him the strength?" I didn't have to say a thing. It's a sweet reminder that the Lord doesn't need us to convince anyone of the truth. In fact, we can't. He alone is the one who reveals truth and revelation about who He is. He may use us as a vessel to say certain things to people about His truth, but He is the one who reveals it to their spirits. All we need to do is speak the truth. There's no need to defend it. Conversely, I've had many instances in which I've tried to talk about the Gospel to others, and they looked at me like I was nuts. No amount of compelling arguments could do a thing to change their minds.

I was able to answer a few other questions about Jesus, and the Lord allowed the Gospel to go forth. The truth is, through my commitment to do the Morrisseys every week, the groundwork had been laid, creating a safe environment and the necessary openness to discuss spiritual matters. "Your skills will accomplish what the force of many cannot." His Word was beginning to unfold. God had my attention. It was time to look up and keep my eyes open.

Assignment #1: Follow through on your word.

Things to Consider:
- Do your words carry weight?
- When's the last time you made a promise to your students and followed through?

Assignment #2: Challenge your students to come up higher.

Things to Consider:
- Is there a small challenge you can present to one of your students to point them in the right direction?
- Offer something that your students desire in exchange for their effort to meet your challenge.

Assignment #3: Earn the right!

Things to Consider:
- What are you going to do to earn the right to speak into their lives?
- When students know that you're for them and want the best for them, they'll allow you to say things to them that others can't.

Chapter 6
New Opportunities

"Eye has not seen, nor ear heard, nor have entered into the heart of man the things which God has prepared for those who love Him."
1 Corinthians 2:9

It was about this time that I noticed an opportunity open to teachers in our surrounding area. It was called Teacherpreneur. I received an email from the district detailing the particulars of the event. They were looking for teachers who had their own ideas to solve some of the problems in education. The idea could be about anything. There were teachers who wanted to build drones, create STEM classrooms, and turn desks into rocking chairs (I really liked this one). At the time, I wasn't even sure if the Morrisseys was the kind of concept they would be looking for, but I figured it couldn't hurt to ask. That's exactly what I did. They had absolutely no problem with my idea. In fact, they seemed intrigued. I decided to apply. The deadline to submit applications was coming up soon, and I liked the fact that they seemed open to people who didn't have a completely fleshed-out idea.

I later realized that this was the entire point. They wanted people who had a raw idea and sought to give them the tools to cultivate it to scale. We would be meeting with the team at various times throughout the summer months to discuss our ideas. These meetings would later culminate with a "pitch" event where we would pitch our idea to a panel of judges/investors who would fund our concept to be implemented during the upcoming school year.

I can remember one of the first meetings we had in the creative space. They allowed members of the community into the space as well to offer feedback as we gave our practice pitches and brainstormed. To date, that afternoon was probably the most enriching professional development experience in all my time in education. They had all types of fun activities, including cornhole and ping pong, for us to do while we brainstormed. I remember thinking, "This must be what it feels like to work at Google." I enjoyed the experience. When it was my turn to pitch, I let it flow.

To my surprise, everyone was intrigued. I got a lot of valuable feedback, but perhaps the most pivotal contribution was from a graphic designer in attendance. She loved my idea and the concept in general. She only had one problem: my design. You see, during my pitch, I showed an example of one of my student's award. It was the award I had been producing on Microsoft Word in Algerian font for the last three months. She offered to make me a professional graphic logo for my award, assuring me it would be ready by the next day. "Cool! Thank you!" I responded.

> You don't have to have everything figured out to move forward.

To her credit, not only was the design breathtaking, but it was delivered to me via email before I woke up the next morning. It looked legit. The design featured a trophy surrounded by a hashed circle with two ribbons extending from both the left and right sides. The left ribbon had the word Math on it. The top of the circle containing the trophy had the word Morrissey wrapped around the top of it. The ribbon on the right had the word Award on it. She had completely remade the Morrissey Award example I had used during my pitch and made me look good. I learned a valuable lesson during that experience. You don't have to have everything figured out to move forward. You only need a vision or, at least, the semblance of one. Let the creative, skilled people come alongside you and turn your rough concept into a masterpiece! They'll make you look good and are more than happy to do it.

I was overwhelmed. I never visualized this concept with such quality before. It was above what I could ask for or think of. And isn't that just like God? As scripture tells us, "Eye has not seen, nor ear heard, nor have entered into the heart of man the things which God has prepared for those who love Him" (1 Corinthians 2:9). He has specific plans for His children, and they are always bigger and better than anything we could come up with on our own. They challenge our sense of what we're capable of and force us to walk forward, knowing that God will come through on our behalf. I think He does this to keep us continually aware that we can't do this on our own. There's no way we can rely on our own abilities. We must remain humble before Him.

Before I knew it, pitch night had arrived. About thirty educators from around the district were selected from approximately sixty applicants to present their ideas in front of a panel of judges and investors. I was slightly nervous. Aside from a few early butterflies, I don't typically shy away from public speaking. I remember eyeing the cue card lady sitting in front with cards showing us how much time we had left in our pitch. I had (and still have!) a tendency to ramble on if left unchecked. We had five minutes to present our idea to the panel. It was on!

The lights came on, and I did my thing. I gave it the best shot that I had. In the end, it wasn't what the judges were looking for. I noticed throughout the event that many of the judges were engineers, construction experts, and people who were used to building physical things. Nearly all the winners were inevitably teachers who pitched ideas to build things. Though my idea was a new way of doing things, the concept was too abstract. The judges couldn't handle or touch what I was building. I wasn't surprised when my name wasn't called. But my efforts were not a failure. I always say, "You don't have to win American Idol to get a contract." By the end of the event, I received two job offers at other schools and made a couple of good contacts for future funding opportunities. *Cool!* I thought.

When it was all said and done, I received a free logo to enhance my idea, gained confidence, and made connections with the right people to help advance my cause. One connection proved life-changing. I received an email from one of the coordinators of the event about a man she felt could help my cause. He had a sterling reputation in town, primarily for establishing one of the most charitable foundations in the area. His work helped build up much of Chattanooga's transformation over the previous twenty years. He was responsible for investing millions of dollars into the community. When I say millions, I mean *millions*. I would later find out that he was personally responsible for growing his non-profit organization from a table and phone outfit to one having over 115 million dollars in assets and awarding more than $300,000 a week to various endeavors.

I knew none of this when I strolled into his office at my scheduled appointment time. I knew enough to know he was kind of a big deal but didn't feel intimidated until he asked me to take a seat. He had an air of confidence about him like no one I had ever met before. You could feel it. He gave off the vibe that his time was extremely precious. I quickly racked my brain to search for ways to communicate concisely and clearly. He had scheduled thirty minutes for me, and I got the sense he wouldn't afford me a second longer.

"Mr. Morris, what can I do for you?" he asked politely.

"Hhhh...hi Mr. Cooper," I stuttered. "Thank you for your time. I'm a math teacher at a local high school with a game-changing idea to engage students." I blurted.

> "That's the reason why twenty years from now, one of your students isn't going to commit suicide!"

I went on to unload my story on him and held nothing back. I didn't know what to expect. I figured I'd tell my story and find out. About halfway through my story, Mr. Cooper interrupted me. We were looking at several examples of awards I had given my students over the past few months. We stumbled upon one case that got his attention. It was an award I described as the "Worth and Value" Award. On it was a picture of a sparkling diamond with a tag that read, "Look how precious it is." I had wanted the student receiving it to know that she was unique and precious in God's eyes. She was struggling with a myriad of insecurities and needed that encouragement. "That's the reason why twenty years from now, one of your students isn't going to commit suicide!" he exclaimed. *Whoa!* I thought. I wasn't even considering that kind of response. I was just trying to see if I could secure some funding to buy little gifts to go along with the awards. God was doing such deep work. A deep work despite me, not because of me. Ephesians 2:10 says, "For we are His workmanship, created in Christ Jesus for good works, which God prepared beforehand that we should walk in them" (NKJV). I was walking into some good works… works with immeasurable impacts on the purposes of Heaven and the Kingdom of God.

We went on to discuss the various problems in education from his vantage point. Mr. Cooper had a way of cutting through the jargon and identifying the root of the issue using very few words. "They don't advertise!" he exclaimed. "I believe it's because they don't have anything to offer of considerable value, and therefore, there is nothing to advertise. In education, they continually do the same things over and over and then complain every few years about needing more funding." He then went on to give an example using a car company as an analogy.

"It's like a car company that fifty years ago made a really good black truck. The truck was nice and served its purpose then, but it never evolved. What if I'd like to look at an SUV or a sedan? What if I'd like the same truck but in a different color? Nope, your only option is the same black truck for fifty years. Furthermore, as I said earlier, they don't advertise. If I want to see the one black truck that they sell I need to go inside the store. There's no billboard, TV commercial, or online inventory to search. That's public education. It's not as if there's a shortage of generous wealth around. It's that the wealthy don't see public education as a good investment because they see virtually no return on their investment. And we can't fire them because education is required by law."

His words weren't nice nor delicate, but I knew they were right. You don't take a foundation from a balance of $0 to having over $115 million in assets in under twenty years without knowing a thing or two. His words carried weight when he spoke. In many ways, I felt like my thirty minutes spent with Mr. Cooper taught me more than several years of instruction from many of my teachers. "Chris, this could become part of a national study!" he added. The conversation went better than I could have ever imagined. He told me that I was a person he would be willing to invest in. We agreed to have an ongoing "as-needed" arrangement for funding. He sent a check to my school for a few hundred dollars for the express purpose of funding my program with the understanding that I could call for more if needed.

The experience was great. But he wouldn't let me go on my way before making me promise that I would read a book he endorsed during our conversation. It was an autobiography by a man with an incredible rag to riches story who lived in town. Mr. Cooper emphasized the power of positive thinking and backed it by citing this book called *When Want-to Becomes Have-to* by Gary Highfield. Like I said before, Mr. Cooper had a way about him. When he said to jump, you jumped. When he told me to read this book, I determined to read several chapters that evening. However, I couldn't put it down. There are only two or three books I've read from cover to cover in a couple of days. This was one of them. It was so raw and real. The author would mention streets and landmarks in town that I was very familiar with as he detailed his early struggles growing up in poverty and the effect that it had on his life. I still recall a quote he often gave in the text, "What's possible is possible for me." Once he even broke the word IMPOSSIBLE into two words: I'M POSSIBLE. That was impactful to me.

It was as if I was changing from the inside out as I read through the pages of his story. To this day, outside of the Bible, I can't recommend a better book to read if you need an inspirational pick-me-up. One of the things Mr. Cooper made me promise him after our meeting was that after I read the book, I think of a student that I could give it to as a reward for winning one of my Morrissey Awards. Little did I know at the time that the Lord was about to put me in a position to provide the entire school with a copy of the book.

Assignment #1: If you have a raw idea, explore it!

Things to Consider:
- What ideas have you brushed off that you should give serious consideration?
- What excuses have you used not to explore them?

Assignment #2: You don't have to have it all figured out to move forward.

Things to Consider:
- God leads us one step at a time. "Your word is a lamp to my feet and a light to my path" (Psalm 119:105 NKJV).
- He generally only shows you the next step. You won't see the following steps until you take the first one. That's walking by faith.

Assignment #3: Don't rely on your own abilities; rely on God!

Things to Consider:
- If you're truly walking by faith, you won't be led on a path where you can accomplish things in your strength. The path will humble you and remind you that only God can bring your dreams to pass (See 2 Corinthians 12:9). Trust in Him!
-

Assignment #4: You don't have to win American Idol to get a contract!

Things to Consider:
- I didn't win the Teaching Competition but still got connected to someone who could fund my idea.
- Not everything that looks like a failure on the surface is one! With God, failure is victory in disguise!

Chapter 7
A Book and a Plan

"What's possible is possible for you"
Gary Highfield

The book was written in a way that I felt could relate to many of our students. The author knew what it was like to come home to no food and bullet holes in the walls. He knew what it was like to move a lot and walk home from school. Chaos and instability were the norms for him. The read helped me understand what life was like for many of our students and helped me become more sensitive and empathetic. It also helped me better understand the mindset of many of my students and feel better prepared to teach them. Heck, the author even knew what it was like to be homeless for a few years during middle school. All these experiences and more uniquely qualified his story to minister to the student body at my high school.

About two months after my conversation with Mr. Cooper, I decided to drop by a local coffee shop on the way home. While I was waiting in line to order, I noticed a familiar-looking man sitting at one of the tables in the corner of the shop. I kept looking his way with a nagging feeling that I had met him before. Hopefully, he wouldn't notice me staring at him before it finally clicked in my mind. It was Gary Highfield, the author of

When Want-to Becomes Have-to! He had a copy of his book lying on the table, which helped me realize where I had seen him before. Immediately, I left my place in line and approached him at his table. "Hi, Mr. Highfield! My name is Chris. I just wanted you to know that I read your book in two days. I couldn't put it down." I let him know that I was a math teacher at one of the local high schools and his eyes lit up. "I've been trying for months to get in touch with a decision-maker at that high school," he said. Mr. Highfield went on to tell me that he had convinced a local business owner to buy a copy of his book for every student at my high school, and he was trying to help the school.

We must have talked for hours. He was on a mission to help the students in the Chattanooga area and had recently left his job at a bank to start a nonprofit named after his book called the *Want To Foundation*. The goal of the organization was to inspire disenfranchised youth with his story and connect them with mentors from the community to provide the kids with a loving, caring adult who would guide them. As the Lord would have it, I happened to be teaching an elective course that year that provided me a great deal of flexibility and autonomy. I was certain that our principal would let me do a book study with that class as a sort of pilot opportunity to see if we should spread it out to the entire school. Mr. Highfield was ecstatic, and I was excited too!

The next day, I was in the principal's office telling the story and proposing the idea. Her response went exactly as I thought it would. "Let's get enough books and do the study in your Contemporary Issues class, and if it goes well, we'll do it for the whole school!" *Wow*, I thought. *It's on!* I informed Mr. Highfield as soon as school was out that day, and he lit up like a Christmas tree. "You did it!" he repeated over and over. "All this time, I was trying to get in touch with the principal, and a math teacher was the solution all along." For him, it was the beginning of his nonprofit becoming a reality.

With my principal's blessing, I decided to make reading Mr. Highfield's book a 4th quarter end of semester project. It would culminate with a class presentation about how the book related to each student personally. Mr. Highfield allowed me to have twenty copies of his book to use in my class with the hopes that he could supply the rest of his copies to the entire school afterward. Knowing the kids, I decided it was wisest to require them to read the book during class. Most of the kids had horrible study skills. I knew if I made reading the book a homework assignment, half of the class wouldn't read it. If I had them read the book during class, I could ensure they were reading it during that period, at least.

That's the approach I took. It worked well. At times they fussed and whined, but eventually, they would get over themselves and start reading. It was great! Not only did the kids get to learn something meaningful, but I got some much-needed teacher prep time added to my day. I decided to have the students read two chapters at a time while they took notes in journals that I provided them for the project. I instructed the kids to walk up to the board and jot down on poster board any takeaways or personal connections they had with Mr. Highfield's story. It was amazing! Several of the kids wrote down that they too had not met nor seen their father in years. Others had family members who had committed suicide, and that stood out to them. I remember one girl who shared with the entire class that she had just found out that she had a sister who was a couple of years younger than her from a relationship that her father had kept secret from her side of the family. For many of the students, the book study became a very cathartic experience. These types of dynamics helped me to better understand the family constructs

> It was as if the students were walking through the halls every day with huge boulders strapped to their backs

of my students and explained some of the apparent dysfunction I witnessed day in and day out. It was a wonder many of the kids could keep their heads up, let alone do their classwork.

It was as if the students were walking through the halls every day with huge boulders strapped to their backs. The heaviness was written all over their faces. Why did I not see it before? Perhaps I didn't want to see. Maybe it was just easier not to know anything about their personal lives. That way I wouldn't have to do anything about it. Whatever my reasons were before, I no longer had any excuses. God placed me in this school for His purpose, and that purpose was becoming more and more clear to me. We couldn't keep concentrating our efforts on dragging the kids through the state standards in hopes that their standardized test scores would increase by a few points. As Mr. Cooper had put it, "The kids are suffocating, and they need air." We needed to intrinsically reach these kids and give them the hope that what's possible was also possible for them.

For two months, we progressed through the book study and became closer as a class. As planned, for the final project, the students gave an oral presentation about what they got out of Mr. Highfield's story. It was clear that a couple of students merely went through the motions, but the majority opened up and fostered real open discussions. As anyone who's ever taught for a year or more knows, the end of a semester is always crazy. Teachers are rushing to get their grades calculated and entered into the computer system. Students are pestering their teachers, trying to get makeup work done at the last minute. Amid the chaos, my boss did manage to track me down, asking how the book study went.

> "The kids are suffocating, and they need air."

"It went wonderfully," I replied.

"Good!" she said. "Why don't you tell Mr. Highfield to order books for the whole school? Let's do the book study school-wide!"

Elated, I quickly agreed and called Mr. Highfield that afternoon. He couldn't believe his ears. "You did it! You did it!" he kept saying over and over. "And just think... all this time I was trying to contact a principal, and it was a math teacher I needed the whole time."

For Mr. Highfield, this was great news. It was the beginning of the realization of his dream to get his book into the local high schools and hopefully begin his mentorship program. He knew these kids needed help, and he was on a mission to do something about it. For myself, it was another witnessing of one of God's miracles. A few months prior, I simply wanted to give a single copy of the book to just one student, and now we were giving a copy to every student in the school—nearly 900 copies! I couldn't help but think about the story in the New Testament about how Jesus was able to feed a crowd of 5000 with just five loaves of bread and two fish. The principle then is the same one for us now. Give me what you have, God says, and I'll multiply it in ways you would not believe. What is it that you have? It could be your time, a few dollars, or even a book. If you determine in your heart to sow that thing, whatever it may be, into the kingdom, the King of kings will multiply it and overwhelm you in the process.

I'll never forget the sight of Mr. Highfield pulling up to the school in his Nissan Altima packed to the hilt with 900 plus copies of his book. There wasn't a square inch of space he didn't utilize in the modest-sized sedan. I recruited a handful of guys from my second-period class to help grab box after box and stack them in the corner of my classroom. Let's just say it took a while. My room became the unofficial storage unit for his books until a better location could be confirmed. Thinking back, I'm not sure that a better location was ever confirmed. There may still be a few copies in my old classroom! The principal had each elective teacher escort his or her class to my room for the students to get their copies of the book. It was organized chaos. Okay, just chaos. But the students each received a copy, and that's what was exciting.

The principal tried to make every teacher lead a book study that year, but most of the teachers didn't. It didn't matter. Many of the students were reading the book for themselves, and truthfully, those were the students who were meant to receive the book in the first place. It was the kind of read that would hit you with just the right truths at just the right time. Not every student was mature enough yet for the richness of his story, but many were. Certain chapters meant different things for different kids. I believe the Holy Spirit was working specifically and individually with each young person through the pages of that story. It had a way of bringing up subjects that were sensitive but forced the reader to deal with them for perhaps the first time. And isn't that how God deals with us? He gently points out issues and things in our lives so that we might be set free from the bondage of those areas. We can't deal with all these issues at once, so He walks us through them one step at a time, one issue at a time. He's being loving in that way.

Conversely, the devil points out our weaknesses in a way that brings with it condemnation. The Bible refers to him as the "accuser of the brethren." His goal is to torment us and get us to turn away from the only One who can heal us. The Holy Spirit points out our weak areas to bring awareness to their crippling effects and lead us into fullness and freedom. The Lord allowed me to play a small part in His work to bring the kingdom of heaven into the lives of the students at my school. It was as if God used my Contemporary Issues class as the last stick of dynamite needed to break open the dam and let His healing flood waters pour through.

"I'm putting together an army," Mr. Highfield told me.

"What do you mean?" I asked.

"My mentors," he replied. That's how he referred to his volunteers. Mr. Highfield was seriously connected. He knew people from all different backgrounds and areas of expertise. He was convinced that they could help him inspire the youth at the high school. Over the course of the school year, Mr. Highfield recruited engineers, doctors and nurses, business owners of all kinds, financial experts, and many more professionals ready and willing to come alongside his mission. By the start of the following school year, he planned to start his mentoring program at our high school, making a difference, and touching lives.

Assignment #1: You've got to get in tune with your kids.

Things to Consider:
- ➤ Do you have any idea what your students are going through?
- ➤ Do you know what they're dealing with?

Assignment #2: Don't be so concerned with your day to day responsibilities that you miss the opportunity to influence lives.

Things to Consider:
- ➤ Jesus stated that the Kingdom of God is at hand. In other words, something deeper and much more profound is going on all around us, but you can't enter in unless you take your eyes off your agenda and place them on the needs of others.

Assignment #3: Get Proactive

Things to Consider:
- ➤ Propose a plan before one is given. If you do, you can control your future and make it work for you. If you don't, someone else will propose a plan for you, and it won't be the future you want to live.

Assignment #4: Sow your seed.

Things to Consider:
- ➤ The Bible says that the Lord provides seed to the sower (See 2 Corinthians 9:10). I determined in my heart that I was going to sow a book. God multiplied that seed to supply books for the entire school.
- ➤ What is it that you can sow? What's your seed? Why not sow it from the heart and watch God multiply it?

Chapter 8
Expanding the Vision

*"Whether you think you can,
or you think you can't, you're right."*
Henry Wright

    At the end of that year, I finally got a chance to stop and look at the transformation of what God had done in my life as a teacher at that high school. I went from being a pretty selfish, lazy, and immature teacher to a person perfectly positioned to head up real change at that school. It wasn't about me anymore. I was continually looking for ways to notice and uplift the students. God's secret was getting me to the end of myself and allowing me to take a good look at myself in the mirror. It was only then that I could truly go in another direction, watching the Lord do what only He could do in and through me.

    In addition to the book study, my Morrissey Awards were continuing to take off with the students. My reputation continued to establish. Many viewed me as one who cared for and possessed a unique ability to relate with any child at the school. It was all a testament to the Lord's work in me and through me. It was fun and a joy to go to work each week as I began to anticipate with excitement the look on each student's face when

I presented that personalized award. I knew I was on to something and soon got the opportunity to explore the concept in another entrepreneurial way.

One day that year, I received an email from an affiliate with the Teacherpreneur Incubator. They told me about a program from a group called Causeway who was teaching a course for people with an idea or cause that could use some guidance. It was a nine-week course that helped people think through their ideas to see exactly what it was that they were on to and if it had legs. It was a great course that walked you through all the different business entities out there and provided great feedback about how best to incorporate your cause. I learned the difference between non-profits, sole proprietors, LLCs, S-Corps, and many other entities.

The course was also significant in that I was part of a cohort. I got the chance to meet all kinds of people and hear about other great ideas from members of the community, all of whom were very passionate about their causes. The causes varied from financial advisors who were tired of seeing the rampant numbers of predatory lending businesses in the area and desired to establish financial education in the schools, to entrepreneurs with life-saving devices utilized for emergency CPR. We had to go through exercises visualizing who our ideal client or customer was and what our product would look like. It was a valuable exercise for me because I hadn't really thought of the Morrisseys as a business opportunity before. Would my customer be the student or the teacher? Perhaps my customer was the administrator of a school. It took much deliberation, but I finally decided that my customer was the teacher or administrator. He or she was the one who needed desperate help in the school system with students who were apathetic and red tape that seemed paralyzing. He or she was the one who had the most significant effect on students. Sure, students were the ones who would be motivated and positively affected, but they weren't the ones paying for or utilizing the service.

There were a lot of opinions early on pushing me to form my cause as a nonprofit. There were undoubtedly plusses to creating a 501(c)3 nonprofit organization, but I wasn't convinced. It seemed that once you organized as a nonprofit, it was difficult to change to a "for-profit" if you decided to switch directions. Furthermore, you had to have a board of directors who all had to sign off on many of the decisions and the direction of the organization. I didn't even really know what the Morrisseys were yet, let alone which direction I should take. It wasn't until I took the Causeway course that someone looked at my idea and felt that it could be for profit.

Week after week, we chipped away at our ideas, gathering feedback and adjusting. By the end of the course, I walked away with two conclusions. I felt that what I had discovered in the Morrissey Awards was a new model for teaching and that I could act as a consultant for schools and other educational institutions. The second conclusion I came to, with the help of the director of our course, was that I needed to write a workbook or teacher's guide to offer potential customers. I remember the director of the course talking with me, insisting that I have something tangible that my customers could hold in their hands. She said, "In my experience, people won't spend their money unless they can hold something tangible in their hands, like a book." Her advice made sense to me, so I decided to make writing the book a priority. One of the things I felt would work well when writing my book was the case studies that I found in the course workbook.

In the Causeway 9-week course, the workbook we went through contained several case studies with different examples of people who were trying to figure out how to navigate the formation of their businesses or nonprofits. I found these to be extremely helpful and felt that this model would easily fit in my workbook for teachers. By this time, I had created fifty or more Morrissey Awards, each one with a specific story and dynamic behind it. I thought I could easily tell the story behind four or so Morrissey recipients and the particular teacher/student dynamic that existed before and after receiving the award. The idea was to paint a picture nearly any teacher could relate to and show how a challenging relationship with a student could turn around using the model.

Like many people out there, I could get excited and start on a new project or idea with enthusiasm. But like many people out there, it was easy for me to fizzle out and not find the fortitude to finish what I started. Even though I started writing the book immediately, I quickly found myself getting distracted and slacking off on the project after a few weeks. It was around this time that I had a conversation with Gary Highfield, the gentleman behind the mentor program at the school. He was opening up with me about his frustrations but also providing me with insight on how he was able to financially turn things around for his family. With one magic sentence, God used him to reach through the cell phone and shake the apathy right out of me: "I was able to completely change the course of my family tree, but I didn't get there by sitting on my butt and goofing off." I felt both convicted and shaken when he spoke these words. To this day, I don't think Gary had any idea what those words did for me, but I guess he knows now if he's reading this book.

No sooner had I hung up the phone with Gary than I was on my laptop writing my book with conviction and purpose. It was as if I had something inside of me that wasn't there before. I was determined to finish what I had started, no exceptions, no excuses. The book just flowed out of me. I think I finished the book within two weeks of that phone call. The first thing I did once I had written what I needed to say was to contact the very graphic designer that had offered to design my logo for the Morrisseys at the Teacherpreneur Incubator. I trusted her design skills and creativity and knew she'd make me look good. That's one thing I'm thankful to have learned during that time of my life. Most people think you must have every angle thought through and that it must be perfect before you can embark on something. The truth is, nothing well-designed and of quality is ever produced that way the first time. All that anyone needs is a rough idea and persistence. They must get around people who are smarter than they are in certain areas who can help them take a rough concept and turn it into something incredible. What I've found is that the people with the specific skills and know-how who can turn someone's dream into reality are just waiting for that someone with a vision to lay before them. You bring the *what*, and they'll help with the *how*. I believe God is waiting for you to grasp the *what* that he's placed in your heart. He's waiting for you not only to see but *believe* the vision He's placed in your heart. He's waiting for you to take the necessary steps of faith to move forward. He already has the right people in place to come alongside you at just the right time, for you to be used by Him to fulfill His purpose for your life. The old saying, "Whether you think you can, or you can't, you're right," has a lot of truth to it.

What I've found to be true for most people, including myself, is that it's hard to believe God when He tells you some grand plan or accomplishment that He's going to perform through you. It's a whole lot easier to believe God when He speaks of the great things that He's doing for someone else or the great things that someone else is going to do. It's a whole other thing to believe Him when the great things He speaks of pertains to you! One of the reasons I think this can be so difficult to believe is because, when God is speaking to you, He rarely, if ever, tells you about something that you can do without Him. It will usually be something that you have little to no experience doing and have no logical reason to believe that you can accomplish. The reason He does this is that He doesn't want you to have confidence in yourself or your abilities but in Christ alone. You must have more confidence in Christ than in your insecurities. It's a discipline of your faith that must be exercised over time and through experience. You must learn to doubt the *doubt* instead of the *truth* that God told you. I think this is what it means in Philippians 4:13 when it says, "I can do all things through Christ who gives me strength." It's not saying that you can do any ol' thing that you want to. It's saying that whatever the Lord calls you to do, you can do through Him as He empowers you to do it.

> You must learn to doubt the doubt instead of the truth that God told you.

After I laid out the vision before the graphic designer and got her input, she agreed to have the project completed within three weeks. I couldn't wait to see what she would dream up. She did such a great job with the logo design, seemingly making something incredible out of nothing, so I knew she'd package the look of my book in an appealing way. Before I knew it, three weeks had passed. My designer had about twenty copies of my book in hand. She seemed even more excited to show me the book design than I was to see it. *It is perfect!* I thought. One of the things she came up with that I loved the most was her design with the case studies. In true 21st century fashion, she had formatted the case study section to look just like a text messaging conversation between the teacher and student. When the teacher was speaking in the case study, it appeared in a purple text message box. When the student was speaking, it was green. It looked polished, clean, and cutting edge. "I love it!" I told her.

The books were finished just in time. It was just in time because the Lord had allowed me an opportunity to present the Morrissey Award concept to my fellow teacher resident trainees during a summer professional development seminar. I was barely paid a thing, but I was excited, nonetheless, for the opportunity. I thought it could be clever to make Morrissey Awards for the teachers at the seminar. It could be a fun way to present the concept to my fellow educators and give them a feel for what it felt like to receive an award as well. I asked the director to provide me with some personal information on each one of the attendees along with something that was positive about each person. I gave him a week to email this to me, and then I went to work on the awards in much the same way I did when I designed awards for my students.

The idea went over perfectly. It was exciting to see the surprise on each teacher's face when he saw his award. I also had volunteers come up and act out the different roles from the case studies. One teacher would play the part of the student, while the other would play the teacher. I wanted to get them involved as much as possible while translating the value of the concept at the same time. I remember my phone ringing in the middle of my presentation. Fortunately, I had the phone set to vibrate, so it didn't interrupt the proceedings, but I was curious who it was.

After my presentation, I ran to the bathroom to check my voicemail in private. I couldn't believe what I was hearing. It was the principal of a charter school in town. I had completely forgotten about some phone calls I had put out a few weeks back to see if any school would be interested in my character ed program. He was calling about my program and seemed interested in setting up a meeting for implementation. I couldn't believe it! *Wow!* I thought. *There's no such thing as impossible!* I was on a high. I was already excited to have the opportunity to present my concept at the teacher residency event. It was terrific handing out books that I had written

Expanding the Vision

and leading a training. Now a real school opportunity was opening, or so it would seem.

I attempted to call the principal after my presentation that afternoon but was unsuccessful. I left a voicemail and waited with anticipation. Nothing! I waited a couple of weeks just in case something had come up... still nothing. Uggh!!! So irritating. A few days later, I tried again. Still no luck. Eventually, I had to give up the whole notion, at least for the time being. It was time to get ready for the new school year and, once again, the Lord redirected my steps. I was excited about my book and awards model. I remember having coffee with a businessman in town who showed some fascination with my idea and tried to convince me to work for his nonprofit. I wasn't so sure. I didn't see how my model and his venture would fit. But I suppose the flattery of it all felt too good to resist. I met with the gentleman several times before God reminded me of His sovereignty, priorities, and most importantly... timing.

No sooner had I left another coffee shop meeting with this businessman than my eyes landed on a Facebook post from an anointed young pastor. I can't remember the exact phrasing of the post, but it said something like this: "Lord, forgive us for making it about us and not leaning on your leading. We write books and discuss deep things over coffee, but we forget your priorities and pace." The words pierced me like a sword in the heart! I was literally showing the man my book while drinking coffee just moments earlier. I've learned that the Holy Spirit speaks to His children in incredible detail at precisely the right time to direct our steps. Most people would probably write this experience off as coincidence, but I knew better.

> In my excitement over the progress I had made, I had forgotten that I was a part of God's story, and I had to move at His pace, not mine.

In my excitement over the progress I had made, I had forgotten that I was a part of God's story, and I had to move at His pace, not mine. Clearly, I had gotten ahead of myself. I decided to refocus on my growing role at the school—helping Mr. Highfield implement his mentorship program at the school. Just before the beginning of the new school year, we were able to arrange a meeting with the assistant principal to plan out how the mentor program could be implemented. Before I knew what happened, the conversation came back to me. "Mr. Morris, we're okay with moving forward with this... as long as you head it up. We simply don't have the time." I went right to work putting together a digital survey that the entire student body would take to help us find out what career they were interested in. It was a coordinating nightmare, as every class had to be scheduled to use the computer labs to take the survey. When push came to shove, we scrapped the idea and opted to allow the students to take it using their cell phones. I don't know why we didn't think of it earlier. *Everyone has a smartphone these days*, I thought. Even the student who wasn't eating three meals a day had a smartphone at our school. Why not take advantage of the school's "bring your own device" policy and allow the kids to log into the survey link on their cell phones. The few kids who didn't have a device could borrow one from a friend. It only took five minutes to complete, and I knew this would avoid a serious headache.

The cell phone strategy worked great. Before the end of the week, we had a database of 800 plus students broken down into several different categories based on the students' career interests. The next task was to report the results to Mr. Highfield so he could begin galvanizing mentors with backgrounds in those various fields. I also had to coordinate with the guidance counselors at the school so we could organize which homeroom teachers would be overseeing which industry. By law, volunteers were not allowed to be alone with students without a certified teacher or employee monitoring the room.

It was interesting to watch the first few mentors talk to the kids. You could tell that, for many of them, it was the first time they had ever spoken in public. One lady was so visibly nervous and flustered that I thought she might break down in tears. To her credit, she fought through it and managed to make a connection with the kids. She was the owner of a popular pizza restaurant in town. She told the kids of her journey starting the restaurant and how she fought through all the ups and downs to eventually make a great living doing what she loved. Perhaps what stands out most to me was the open love and appreciation she had for her employees. She realized that their attitude, dedication, and hard work were the lifeblood of her business. Her talk showed everyone how important it is to put your people first. If you do, they will take care of your customers. Most importantly, your people will feel valued and cared for with a sense that they matter. They'll take ownership over their work and give you their blood, sweat, and tears.

The mentoring was anything but a smooth process. It was organized chaos every week. Every Wednesday, the mentors would flood the school and wait to be told by the guidance staff which room they would be in to mentor the students. Some days went smoothly, but most days were a mixed bag with some mentoring groups seeming to gel and others struggling to connect. At times, a few mentors failed to show up on the day they promised. Suffice it to say; this did not go over well with some of the guidance counselors and teachers. Anytime you're trying to do something new or different; there will be people who resist and complain. I suppose we're all creatures of habit and prefer to do what's comfortable or what has always been done. The process was anything but smooth, but for me, it always came down to one thing. Were the kids better or worse off doing the mentorship program? They were still better off, the way I saw it. Why would we deprive kids of the opportunity to establish loving, caring relationships with adults who could connect them to more opportunities and a glimpse of hope?

I can remember one instance where a school employee was particularly troubled. He was promised about ten mentors that day, and only six showed up. He was livid. After all, he took the time to schedule where all the students were to go and had selected which groups had which mentor. In his mind, this was inexcusable. The problem was, the people scheduled were volunteers in the business world who often had last-minute things arise, sometimes the night before. I remember one mentor, a nurse, who was scheduled to talk to the kids but went into labor the night before. I tried to explain this to the perturbed faculty members, but they didn't care. To me, last-minute changes were not that big a deal. Just have the teacher assigned to that room watch the kids for twenty minutes and explain what happened. It didn't have to be the end of the world.

Over the year, the mentors got the chance to speak with the entire student body. There were high and low points with the program. Some of the teachers didn't like it, and some loved it. I knew it wasn't perfect, but I knew one thing to be true. The school was better off having the mentors become involved with the students than they would have been if they never showed up at all. I never could understand how anyone could come to any other conclusion other than they were personally inconvenienced. If it was about the students, then you had to see the benefit. If it was about self, then I suppose that was a whole other problem.

Expanding the Vision

Assignment #1: Take steps of faith.

Things to Consider:
- ➢ God's waiting for you to grasp the vision He's planted in your heart.
- ➢ Grasp the vision and act.

Assignment #2: Hang out with Eagles, not Chickens!

Things to Consider:
- ➢ Do your friends and confidants encourage your dreams or detract from them?
- ➢ Who are you hanging around with, and what are they saying to you?
- ➢ Do they expand your vision or limit it?

Assignment #3: Believe Christ more than your doubts!

Things to Consider:
- ➢ I once heard someone say you've got to learn to doubt the doubt. Stop doubting the truth of what God has said and learn to doubt your doubts.
- ➢ Say," I doubt you doubt!"

Assignment #4: Ask yourself a simple question.

The Question:
- ➢ Are my actions helping the kids or not?

Chapter 9
Transformed

"And do not be conformed to this world, but be transformed by the renewing of your mind, that you may prove what is that good and acceptable and perfect will of God."
Romans 12:2 NKJV

Aside from overseeing the mentor program and doing my Morrissey Awards in my classroom, the Lord was doing another profound thing at the school through me. With the success of the Morrissey Awards, the school felt it would be a great idea for us to do this concept school-wide. Mr. Carson, my best friend at work and constant helper, encouraged me to pioneer the effort. He helped me with details and made sure I thought through all the factors. We decided to name a school-wide version of the Morrisseys, what I would call the Valley Awards. We would create a digital form that all teachers could access to nominate their students for an award. Like the Morrisseys, the Valleys were about awarding character improvements and positive strides that students were making in individual classrooms. Once the teachers submitted their nominees, a spreadsheet generated that would allow Mr. Carson and me to select the winners and design the certificates.

After consultation with the administration, we decided it would be best to do the Valley Awards during pep rallies and other school-wide assembly events. The vision was set, and I was pumped! Suddenly, I had gone from being a struggling, apathetic math teacher to one of the primary instruments of the Lord's hand, spearheading monumental change throughout the school. My wheels were turning. I could already see it! We needed to hype up these Valley Awards and get the students excited in anticipation well in advance of the day of the Valleys. About this time, a Bruno Mars song, "Uptown Funk," was beginning to become popular. It was fun, upbeat, and different. I thought this could be the perfect song to introduce the Valleys at the next pep rally. My idea was to orchestrate a sort of flash mob dance routine that only a few students in the school knew about. We could call the dance "Valleytown Funk" and use the routine to get the students excited about the concept.

For the next week, I didn't exactly get a lot of math teaching done. I used about twenty minutes of class time a day to recruit students to be a part of the choreographed dance and practice the dance moves. We had an absolute blast! The black kids showed the white kids (and me!) how to do the "Whip" and a few other popular dances. We found ways to incorporate humor too. No one stole the show quite like Wyatt from first period. He had a kind of Jack Black-Chris Farley-Madonna dance vibe that was hilarious. He danced fearlessly with no shame, which only helped everyone else let loose and crack up at the same time. I decided that we would wait for just the right moment in the routine to unveil Wyatt's solo act before we brought it all together.

The kids were beyond excited. They were stoked! A buzz was starting to permeate throughout the halls of the school as the day of the Valleys approached. A good many of the students knew about the dance, but the rest of them didn't have a clue. I had a few Michael Jackson/Usher moves I had polished over my years in college to introduce the track, as well as all the surprises lined up with the kids ready to join me on the gym floor. Wyatt would come in at just the right time to get the crowd bellowing in laughter. Once again, I must emphasize Wyatt's dance style as a flamboyant mix of Chris Farley and Jack Black. The point is that the routine was without shame and intense. I start laughing every time I think about his ridiculous choreography, just as everyone did who was in our rehearsals.

The Valleys would serve as a fun platform for the kids to let loose a little and really express themselves without the usual classroom constraints. It was a first in the school's recent history. "Sit still!" "Get in your seat!" "Be quiet." Students hear this all day long and are continually having to restrain themselves. I believe that half of the time, kids are misbehaving or refusing to do their work because we don't provide them an outlet which communicates that it's okay to be themselves. They need to learn that there's a time and a place for everything. Sometimes, in education, we need to create that time and place.

Before we knew it, the day of the Valleys was upon us. I was working all week tirelessly, designing the awards for the ceremony and conducting impromptu dance rehearsals with the kids. They were giving us about ten minutes at the end of the pep rally to unveil the concept to the student body. All the students involved needed to know their cues and be in their positions. I planned to be the only one at the center of the court dancing to the intro to "Uptown Funk." I had on a blazer and jeans and made it appear like I was a one-man show. Suddenly, ten to fifteen students ran from various positions all over the gym and joined me at the center of the court doing the whip and other choreography in perfect unison. The rest of the students went crazy with excitement trying to figure out what was going on. Just before our routine was starting to get old in the minds of the student body, Wyatt came rushing out to center court, Jack Black style, completely bringing down the house. The whole school was laughing and cheering him on. Perhaps the highest moment was when Wyatt and another student randomly went into a dance-off at center court going back and forth. It was a blast!

After Wyatt and his competitor's dance-off routine, the rest of the flash mob joined in with the rest of our choreography to hit it home! The student body ate it up. The dancing students had a blast and cherished the memory we all shared. The funny thing was, I don't think we ever rehearsed the routine as well as we all performed it that day. There were holes in the routine that I was afraid we would not be able to pull off, but somehow, everyone was on point. There were dorky kids who never seemed to be able to grasp the concept of "the whip" but magically got their acts together and stayed in rhythm. The kids communicated and came together in unison in a way that they never seemed able to do it when it came to their studies. I mean, honestly, half of those kids had never even come to the rehearsals but succeeded because they were told what moves to do from other students. The mission was a huge success! The Valleys were exciting, not only for the winners of the awards but also for the entire student body. It was a fun event that was about the kids, and they knew it! Everyone wanted to win an award, so I knew we teachers finally had leverage in the classroom if only we could grab hold of it. From now on, I simply had to remind the students that I was thinking of nominating them for an award and nine times out of ten they would shape up their behavior, giving me an easier time at work. Getting the other teachers to understand this was a bit of a challenge, but some of them were grasping the concept. I think that video of the dance went viral more so than any video posted on social media in the school's history. The following day, nearly every class requested to watch the video of the Valley dance. How could I say no? I had to oblige. It really seemed to help the classes come together. They could be themselves, but they were also more willing to play my game at the same time.

The school year moved along, and there was a buzz amongst the students that wasn't there before. Kids were excited and asking me every day when we were going to have another Valleys. I told them to slow their horses. It wouldn't happen until it was time for another pep rally. I was a part of a committee that was tasked to think of positive behavioral support ideas for the school at that time. Mr. Carson and I would pretty much think of Valley ideas throughout those meetings. I remember an idea hitting me like a ton of bricks in the middle of one of those committee meetings. "We should put the kids on a billboard!" I blurted aloud. A few moments later, Mr. Carson turned and looked my way, saying, "You know, under the public service announcement provision, Fairway will allow you to use a billboard for just $160." That was amazing! It was also very typical of Mr. Carson. Looking back, I can see now how God always used him to be the encouragement in my ear telling me to go for it! I would have an idea, and Carson would quickly start telling me how it could be done, sorting out the details. Praise God for him! At lunch break, Carson was already on the phone with Fairway verifying the possibility of putting the Valley Award winners on a billboard near the school. Sure enough, because we were a school initiative, we could get it for $160.

I couldn't believe it. It was altogether possible. I was sure I could convince Mr. Cooper from the foundation to let us use some of the funds for the billboard. He agreed, and we went for it. I didn't know the first thing about photography, pixel sizes, or how to submit billboard images. I talked back and forth with Fairway personnel before finally finding a guy in the right department who could help me. He asked me to email him pictures of the students we wanted to display, with a copy of our logo. He would do the rest. Carson and I quickly got to work getting the students who we thought showed the greatest transformation to get media release forms signed by their parents. I took their pictures on my iPhone and emailed them over to the billboard company. They told me it would be up at the end of May, just in time for the kids to see them before the end of the school year.

The kids were excited. I was exhausted and excited at the same time. A few weeks later, we got word that the billboard was up on the main road right next to the school. Mr. Carson and I hopped in the car and drove up the road with our heads looking up, trying to see the billboard. Suddenly, it came into view. Amazing! It was huge. The billboard looked as legit as any other company advertisement in sight. Four of our students were smiling right under the Valley logo with their character traits listed underneath their photos. Within a month, a crazy notion I had in a committee meeting was a reality displayed for the entire area to see. What a message to send to our students! The seemingly small steps they chose to make in the right direction could lead to them being in a prominent position, a position usually reserved for the select few. It was a statement proving that they mattered. It was a way to show the community a side to our students that they had never seen before. Through this process, everyone's perception of each other, community-wide, was becoming more positive and uplifting.

When you see someone in a positive light, even if that person is a bit rough around the edges, it opens the door for love to take root between individuals. You get a glimpse of the real person, the person he or she was created by God to be before sin tainted their true image. You get a glimpse of who that person could be. When people feel that you see them this way, they're inspired to live up to your positive perception of them. This is what God was doing through this process. It's what the Lord was allowing me to be a part of. Honestly, this is the way God sees each one of us who are His children. He doesn't see the sin-tainted, screwed up image we see in each other. Through Christ's sacrifice for us on the cross, He sees us as He sees his only Son. He sees the finished product the way we will be one day and the way we were meant to be.

When someone sees you this way, you can't help but change. Shame disappears, and you can see clearly again. When your flaws aren't reflected in the other's eyes, it frees you! It allows you to turn away from destructive behavior and towards grace. Praise God! He's showing us how to love each other. Shame is a powerful factor in the lives of many students today. Curtis Thompson, author of the best-seller *The Soul of Shame*, presents evidence of shame's connection to the prefrontal cortex of the brain, which is largely responsible for judgment, decision-making, and problem-solving. As a high school math teacher of a culturally diverse student body, I found many students who struggled with these issues. I believe that the Lord was using these awards to tear down the strongholds of shame and its debilitating effects. If it's true that judgment, decision-making, and problem-solving are hindered due to shame, why aren't we taking a harder look at it? Wouldn't that resolve a significant amount of the issues we see in our schools today or in our society for that matter?

> When you see someone in a positive light, even if that person is a bit rough around the edges, it opens the door for love to take root between individuals.

Shame is defined by a painful feeling of humiliation or distress caused by the consciousness of wrong or foolish behavior. Individuals who are conscious of their inadequacies can feel a continual sense of embarrassment and indignity. From the perspective of many kids I've taught, the school environment is a reminder of the assumed reality that they're not good enough or subpar. It's a place of shame for many students. No wonder there's such little motivation to apply themselves or put forth an effort. They see no point in even trying because of the constant sense of shame they feel. Over the years, I've heard statements from students like:

- "Nothing I can do or say is going to make a difference, so why risk being humiliated or reminded that I'm a loser!"
- "I don't care about life in general, so why should I play your game?"

For far too many students, the present-day testing schedules and grading structures serve as a constant reminder of the shame that they feel.

- "I'm not good enough."
- "I'm a disappointment."
- "There's no hope for me."

These statements ring loud in the minds of kids throughout the country. If we continue this downward trend of ignoring the shame, we only serve to demotivate individuals instead of inspiring them.

The Lord was indeed doing a work in me and through this process. He was showing me how He sees people, how to love them, and how to build them up. He was teaching me to ignore the shame and see a person's spirit. It's about calling people up into who they were meant to be. And this was a practical way to do it.

By the following year, I was primed and ready to continue walking out these initiatives. In addition to doing my weekly Morrissey Awards, I oversaw the scheduling of the mentor program and spearheaded the periodic Valley school-wide awards. My hands were full, but in a good way. God gave me the grace to get it all done. I loved my job! I couldn't wrap my mind around it. How did I go from absolutely hating my job to loving it? It was the same job. The truth was I had changed. My perspective and purpose had changed. I was no longer reactive to the chaos going on around me but proactive in the work I felt called to do. It made all the difference. My value in the eyes of administration had increased so much that they stopped asking me to do a lot of the tedious tasks many of the teachers hated doing. The thought was, "Chris is already doing so much.

We'll leave him alone." The funny thing for me was that what I was doing didn't really feel like work for me. I loved it. Wow, God!

So many people think that they must make money doing something they love, that that is the secret to a happy life. The truth in Christ is, if you obey Him, even if it's hard at first, if you persevere, He will show you why He created you. And the best part of it is, you'll love it! He can give you new desires. Suddenly, you'll start wanting things you never wanted before. And these things will line up with God's will. Suddenly, you're not fighting against God anymore but lined up with Him, wanting the same things. When you pray in this state, you'll get what you ask for because you're praying God's will. Some of you are frustrated because it seems that God isn't answering your prayers or giving you what you want. Ask God to give you new desires. When He does, it won't be frustrating. You won't be warring against the Spirit. You'll ask and have because you won't be asking amiss (James 4:3). What would your life look like if the things you desired and asked for were the same things God desired and wanted to grant you? Would it not be exhilarating? Your prayers would consistently be answered, and peace would rule in your heart. You wouldn't be at war with yourself, and you would notice God's presence with you throughout the day.

The fantastic news for believers in Jesus is that this is entirely possible for each one of us. It only takes surrender and a willingness to ask the Lord to change your desires. Don't you think God would answer that prayer? That prayer is not amiss. That prayer is spot on. You will no longer want to look at dirty things or gossip or complain. You'll be a new creation, and you'll feel the difference. It's weird at first. Freedom feels strange to those who are accustomed to living in bondage. However, once you adjust, you'll realize what you've been missing out on all your life… amazing grace and abundant life.

Assignment #1: Disarm shame by finding the good

Things to Consider:

➢ We don't need to point out people's flaws as much as we think we do. More likely than not, they're fully aware of them. Pointing them out only makes matters worse.

➢ When you look at a person, ignore the flaws! Instead, look for the good and speak to it. Tell people their true value and their positive qualities. You'll be amazed by the results.

Assignment #2: Ask God for new desires

Things to Consider:

➢ If our desires are evil, why would God grant them to us?

➢ What we need are new and Godly desires.

➢ God gives us His desires. Those are the desires of our heart, referred to in Psalm 37:4.

Chapter 10
A Surprising Breakthrough

*"A goal should scare you a little
and excite you a lot."*
Joe Vitale

Among the many notable works of the Lord, that year was the transformation I was privileged to witness in my Contemporary Issues class. I was leading another book study of *When Want to Becomes Have to* by Gary Highfield. Ray Shelton was the only teenager in the class who wasn't engaged or paying attention. Yes, every student was locking eyes with me except Ray who was drooling on the desk, drifting fast asleep in the third row. "Ray, sit up!" I yelled. Ray lifted his head for a minute before falling right back to sleep just moments later. We repeated this process several times before I gave up and decided to count my losses. *Unbelievable!* I thought. I was busting my tail to make this class engaging and provide valuable inspiration, and he couldn't care less.

I was discussing the importance of setting goals and writing them down with the students, providing them with convincing data to support its importance. All the students seemed to appreciate the lesson except Ray. His behavior didn't surprise me. Nearly every teacher who ever had the pleasure of teaching Ray had similar stories to tell. "He's no good!"

they would say. "His whole family's that way!" It was hard to argue based on my limited experience thus far. I had just about given up on the lad altogether when I noticed something shocking that evening. I was checking my class Facebook page to post the week's Morrissey winners when I noticed a student post on the homepage. It was from Ray. On it, he had written something that I never saw coming. "Mr. Morris is always talking about how important it is to write down your goals, so here I go. I want to design my own shoe!"- Ray.

I couldn't believe my eyes. The day I was pleading with the kids to write down their goals was the exact day that Ray's head was lying in a pool of his own drool. I didn't think he heard a word that came out of my mouth, let alone took it to heart. The crazy thing was, he was the only student out of twenty kids who took me up on my challenge and wrote down a goal at all. Even though Ray never took the time to write down his goal on his paper during class, he still found a way. *A social media post is still writing*, I thought. Mr. Highfield was always stressing the fact that things start to work out once you take the time to write your goals down. Little did I know how quickly this truth would begin to manifest.

The next morning, I attended a fundraising event hosted by Gary's mentor program. At the lunch event, he introduced some of his supporters and board members. One of his board members was a man who owned a shoe company. Ray and his goal immediately came to mind. *I need to meet this man and tell him about Ray*, I thought. When the opportunity presented itself, I introduced myself to him and told him all about Ray and his goal of designing his own shoe. He was gracious and agreed to meet Ray soon. I was elated. *I can't believe this. I can't wait to tell Ray!* I thought. *I know, I'll make him a Morrissey award as a way of celebrating his goal-setting and telling him what transpired!*

That's precisely what I did. I found graphic photos of shoes and design themes and wrote up the award. It went a little something like this:

The Goal-Setter Award goes to Ray Shelton for Making a Goal and Writing It Down! I had the reason displayed. *"Ray, not only did you set a great foundation for your own life, but you were a shining example for the student body*

A Surprising Breakthrough

at large! When you make up your mind to start working on yourself, things start to work out! I believe you're going to accomplish your goal. Let's design your shoe!" His reward was to get a meeting with the shoe company owner.

Ray ate it up. You could see the life beaming in his eyes. Let's just say, Ray didn't take a nap that class period. I don't think he took one for the rest of the quarter. After meeting with the shoe company owner, Ray began the most significant turnaround I've ever witnessed in the classroom setting. Suddenly, Ray possessed a drive and a reason to study that he never had before. His English teacher approached me one day after school to tell me about his amazing turnaround. She said Ray now leads his class in grade average and daily begs her to get his grades done so he can see where he stands. This is the same student who, one year prior, had failed her class. "I think it's because he won a Morrissey award," she told me. I felt it was a combination of meeting the shoe company owner, our Contemporary Issues lessons, and the awards. Ray was a seeker of attention and admittedly loved getting awarded in front of the school body. I knew if we could continue to fan the flame, he'd jump through a brick wall for us if we asked him to.

Stories like Ray's were a joy to see. Another similar story that occurred revolved around a girl named Kierra. In my eyes, Kierra was a hot mess. A lovable hot mess, but a mess, nonetheless. She had the attention span of a gnat, about ten seconds at best. She was easily distracted and emotionally immature. However, one endearing quality she possessed was her ability to laugh at herself. It was as if she knew as much as I did that she was ridiculous. One day, I asked Mr. Highfield to be a guest speaker in my third period. Most of the kids were stoked to have a break from learning math and were bright-eyed and attentive. That is... everyone but Kierra. True to form, about five minutes into Mr. Highfield's presentation, Kierra was asleep, drooling on the desk much like Ray had been in the Contemporary Issues class. I snapped my fingers and tapped her shoulder numerous times to avoid embarrassment, but there was no hope. Kierra was just being Kierra.

Like Ray, I assumed Kierra wasn't listening to a word Mr. Highfield was saying. Mr. Highfield mentioned to the students that he was having another fundraiser dinner for the mentor program downtown and encouraged any kids who wanted to go to come. Later that day, after I finally got the chance to pull out of the parking lot to head home, I noticed Kierra leaning over the railings of the school shouting my direction. I rolled my window down to hear what she wanted to say. "Mr. Morris, where is that event with that man going to be?" Once again, I couldn't believe it. Kierra heard what Mr. Highfield was saying and wanted to attend. I gave her the address and, sure enough, she showed up at the event just a few hours later dressed in a sparkling gown.

All in all, ten to fifteen of my students showed up that night. They were excited about the mentor program and meeting influential people who wanted to help them. They got to meet businessmen, people from the music industry, and other professions. They got the chance to listen to a keynote speaker who had climbed Mount Everest. The title of the talk was called "What's Your Everest?" I remember earlier that morning when Mr. Highfield was still speaking to my class, watching him go around the room and asking each student what they wanted to do. When he got to Kierra, she responded with "singer." Everybody giggled at her response. It was interesting, however, that at the event that evening, she met a man who had a son in the music industry. I believe he was a studio producer in Atlanta. I didn't think much of it at the time. There were several professionals in attendance all talking with the kids. It wasn't until a few weeks later, after Kierra had been out of class a couple of days, that the topic came back up for discussion. I was in the middle of teaching when Kierra interrupted me. "Mr. Morris!"

"Not now Kierra, I'm trying to cover this unit."

"But Mr. Morris, it's important."

"Hush, not now." It wasn't uncommon for Kierra to interrupt me with annoying questions, so I didn't pay her any attention. "Mr. Morris!!!" Kierra interrupted again.

"What is it, Kierra?" I yelled.

"Don't you want to know why I was out the last couple of days?"

"Not really," I said jokingly.

"I was in Atlanta recording an album."

"Whatever you say, Kierra," I responded. I was about to continue my lesson when I saw the other girls nodding their heads in agreement with Kierra. Suddenly, I remembered the gentleman she met at the fundraising dinner. "You mean…" I began.

"Yes!"

"You recorded an album?!?" I said. By now, I was shouting.

"I called the number on the business card he gave me at the dinner and his son agreed to coach me on my singing and helped me record a demo." I couldn't believe my ears. Kierra...Kierra…. Kierra of all people did this.

"You did what?" I yelled again in disbelief. *What is going on?* I thought. *This is incredible!* "You just called him up?"

"Yes," she said.

"How did you get there?" I wondered. "I know you can't drive."

"My dad drove me," she responded. There must be something about these napping students. Perhaps that's how they listen best. "I'm just as proud of you as I am shocked," I told her. I guess the lesson behind these experiences was not to write off anybody. Sometimes the least likely are the ones who accomplish the most. Maybe it's the ones who are bold enough to sleep in your class who are the very ones who are brave enough to do just about anything.

To be honest, I wasn't even sure if Kierra could sing. In fact, I was pretty sure that she couldn't. But I didn't care. I was just so proud of her for having the courage to try and get the experience. Several students in that class could sing ten times better than Kierra and didn't have the courage to call the music producer, even though they met the same contact at the fundraiser. How many of us miss out on opportunities right in front of us because we're just too afraid to go for it… too scared to make a call and ask questions. We have not because we ask not!

I was also proud of the example she set for her classmates. She showed that the things we were talking about weren't just idle talk but real truths. It made an impression on her friends and classmates who made a habit of thinking of reasons why they couldn't do certain things. It made an impression on me as her teacher and reminded me not to prejudge my students. Kierra went on to record at the producer's studio once a month for a few months before eventually deciding that singing wasn't for her. I think her increased confidence from this experience served her well.

In addition to these accounts was the continual evolution of the school-wide Valley Awards. The kids were buying in more and more each time we conducted the ceremony. Students from other classes would stop me in the halls, asking if they could win an award or be a part of the next flash mob dance routine. It was fun. After Wyatt and the crew broke the ice, everyone wanted to be involved. And it made them want to be in school. One of the realities of working at a challenging school with high poverty rates was truancy. There was a percentage of students who skipped school regularly. Faculty members had to check on their whereabouts continually. I found it amusing and significant that, whenever word got out that it was the week of the Valleys, many of these truant students would show up to school that week, especially if they thought there was a chance they might win an award. This is the power of recognition and leverage. If you can understand how badly people want something, you can elicit specific behaviors from them that they usually wouldn't perform. **(LEVERAGE)** This is how I understood the power of the Morrisseys and the Valleys to be.

> If you can understand how badly people want something, you can elicit specific behaviors from them that they usually wouldn't perform.

Assignment #1: Don't write off those sleeping kids.

Things to Consider:
- In both examples, the students who appeared to be sleeping in the class were listening the most.
- Are there any sleeping students in your classes that have caused you to lose hope? Hope again!
- Maybe those kids are the bold ones.

Assignment #2: Tap into the power of recognition and leverage.

Things to Consider:
- Have you ever considered how badly people are starved for recognition?
- Have you considered using what people want most to elicit more from them?
- Recognition is leverage. Leverage is the ability to get maximum output with minimal effort.
- You want to have leverage in whatever it is that you do.

Assignment #3: Have your students write down their goals.

Things to Consider:
- A goal is a direction to aim toward.
- If your students are aimless, don't be surprised when they don't go anywhere.
- While you're at it, write down your goals too

Chapter 11
Making a Difference

"To love better you've got to know better."
Christopher W. Morris

All in all, it was an astounding year. It's funny how the school's mascot was the pioneers because I felt like the Lord was allowing me to pioneer all the cultural changes in this season of my life. When attacks came, they didn't last for long, and God always got the victory. I seemed to be able to win over some of the most challenging students when many other teachers had come to their wit's end.

I remember one student, Manuel Martinez. Manuel was a troubled teen with a chip on his shoulder. He was part of a local gang, and some teachers likened the experience of teaching Manuel to walking on eggshells. If Manuel woke up on the wrong side of the bed, expecting him to be the model student was impossible.

One morning, Manuel's ways began to surface. I asked the students to sit in groups of two for a group activity. "I'm not going to work with nobody, Mr. Morris," Manuel exclaimed.

"What do you mean, Manuel? That's not an option. You have to work in pairs today."

"I don't mean no disrespect. I'll do all the work. I'm just not going to work with nobody today," he replied.

After a momentary standoff, I asked Manuel to step out in the hallway for a short conversation. Once outside, he began to explain how he didn't want any trouble and couldn't afford to be suspended. "I'll tell you what. Stay out here a couple of minutes, and then come back in class." I decided that even though Manuel was blatantly disobeying classroom instructions, he was perhaps doing so for noble reasons. Manuel probably knew himself well. He probably knew that he was in a "mood." If he were to work with someone, it was likely that he would lash out at that person. What seemed on the surface to be insubordinate behavior was actually an act of self-awareness and a step toward responsibility.

> What seemed on the surface to be insubordinate behavior was actually an act of self-awareness and a step toward responsibility.

As we had discussed, Manuel came walking into class a few minutes after I returned. To the class, it looked like he had just been chewed out and set straight, but really, he was following through on our deal. He didn't sit in groups, but, to his credit, he worked diligently and was quiet and compliant. I knew by the time I got home that afternoon that I wanted to make Manuel a Morrissey Award and went straight to work. It was a perfect opportunity to give a person, who had probably never received any positive recognition, a breath of life.

I called his award the "Cool Headed" Morrissey Award. It went to him for Outstanding Decision Making and Self Control. I always include a reason section on each award and wrote the following: *"Taking the time to explain to his teacher why he needed some alone time and trying to control his temper for his future good."* His reward was a homework pass and the right to eat snacks in class. I also picked up a stress ball from the local sports store that I thought he could use the next time he had a heated moment. The very next day, when I felt like the students could use a little pick me up, I began playing my Morrissey Award theme music and unveiled the surprise award to Manuel in front of the class.

Making a Difference

It was perfect. He was already having a rough morning. His face looked downcast and was visibly irritated. You could see him trying not to smile when I gave him his award, but even he couldn't help but smirk when I tossed him his stress ball while explaining the reason. From that moment on, I had him. If Manuel was having a hard day or being a little temperamental, I only had to mention the stress ball, and he would laugh and forget why he was mad. I'm convinced if I had not done this process near the beginning of that school year, I would have had an entirely different experience with that young man.

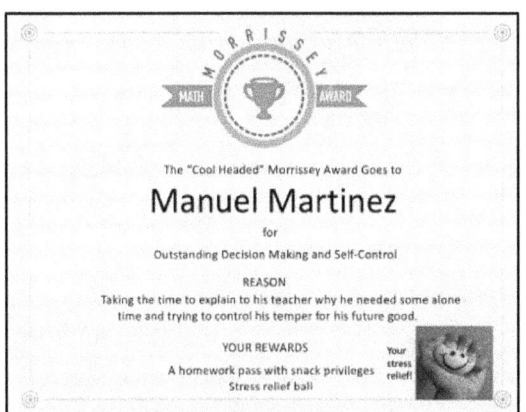

We genuinely liked each other from that point forward. The funny thing was, his other teachers still had a problem with him. He would snap at them, and they would snap right back every time. He was constantly getting in trouble and having to serve in-school suspension, but not in my class. In my class, we could always work it out, and I rarely, if ever, had to write him up all year. It wasn't until the second semester that I realized what a difference, with the Lord's help, I had made.

It was an ordinary mid-week afternoon. I was still at school grading papers and thinking through future lesson plans when Manuel came barging into my classroom. "Mr. Morris, let's do the homework we started today in class." I was startled, not only because a student came barging into my class so late after school but that it was Manuel of all people. I was also equally shocked that he wanted to do math work. This alone was a work of God.

Manuel continued. "I'm sick of this dumb "B" getting in my face, you know. I just walked out of in-school suspension (ISS). I don't even care. Mrs. Spencer kept making me work, and I told her I didn't want to do nothing. She kept getting in my face, so I called her a dumb "B" to her face and walked out. She makes me so mad, you know. So, I decided to come here and get some help with the lesson you taught today. I didn't understand what you were talking about. Show me how to do it!"

It was a lot to absorb. After gathering my thoughts, I came to the following conclusions: 1) Manuel was a troubled person and needed some serious help learning to respond to his environment. 2) How cool was it that he felt safe to come to me and trusted me to confide in? He's even asking to do his math work. It showed me that, even though he had quite a way to go, he did care about his life and his future.

I decided to begin our engagement by complying with his request to go over his homework. We started going over the new formulas and how to utilize them. I knew if we started doing the math, it would take Manuel's mind off his anger, and we could start a meaningful conversation.

After about five minutes or so of explaining how to do the homework, I made my move to talk about the real issue. "So, Manuel, what is it that Mrs. Spencer said that made you so mad?" Manuel went on about how she did this and that, how she rubbed him the wrong way, but he never really said anything substantive. I got the impression that he simply didn't like her, and it was as simple as that. We then shifted the conversation to how he could better respond to situations and people with whom he had issues.

I asked him if he ever prayed. "I talk to God at times," he said.

"He is real and wants you to talk to Him," I replied. I told him how God could help him when it came to his anger and lack of self-control. "Hey Manuel, next time Mrs. Spencer makes you angry, I want you to promise me that you won't just cuss her out. Walk away if you need to and begin praying for God's help. Then, I'd like you to tell me how you're doing each week." We talked back and forth, and eventually, he agreed to give it a try. We even finished the night's homework before he left for the day. *How cool was that?* I thought. It really does come down to relationship. We must genuinely take an interest in others and put the work and time in to develop deeper relationships.

Honestly, that's the only hope for this world. It's the people who take the time and effort to get to know a person who make all the difference. They are the only ones with a chance of influencing others. So few people do this, and we're left with the results. Most people interact with one another on an incredibly superficial level. The bottom line is… you can't love someone if you don't know them. You can attempt to do loving things, but you can't love in a way where they feel it if you don't know them. Isn't that the longing of our hearts? To know and be known? How great is it when someone just gets you? Sure, it can be scary at first to let someone in, but it's such a healthy thing when, at the end of the day, you know a person gets you and is for you. That's where God led me regarding my relationships with Manuel and many other students at that high school. I began to really know them and how they ticked. I knew what buttons to push and which ones to avoid. I learned that Sarah in third block had a five-minute attention span and would need me to call out her name frequently to regain her attention. I knew she wasn't embarrassed by this but was genuinely appreciative of the reminder. I learned that Ashley fared better if I gave her leadership opportunities in class. I learned that Kyle liked to rap, and if I'd give him a few minutes a week to rap in front of his peers, he would bust his tail all week long.

I also learned, at a class-wide level, when my students mentally checked out, and I needed to switch things up or just do something silly. It was about staying in tune with my kids. I learned not to waste my breath teaching when no one was listening. I had them repeat what I had just said to make sure they were listening. Yes, staying in tune was the key. It's much like our relationship with God. We must keep in tune. We need to listen carefully and intently; otherwise, we'll get ahead of Him or behind. It's about doing exactly what He said and not one iota more or less. That's a close relationship. That's an in-tune dynamic that He wants us to have with each other. It's amazing how much greater our capacity is to love when we actually *know* the person we say we love.

> It's incredible how much greater our capacity is to love when we actually know the person we say we love.

I think this is why Jesus repeatedly asked Peter if he loved him. Peter insisted that he loved Him, but Peter didn't know Jesus yet as well as he thought. Jesus, being God, wanted desperately for others to hear of the good news of His sacrifice for them. He wanted to buy back those He had lost and have a relationship with them. If Peter truly knew the heart of Jesus at that moment, he wouldn't have found it so odd for Jesus to request that he feed His sheep. In a way, Jesus was telling Peter how to love Him back. Make no mistake. Telling others about Jesus speaks God's love language. He feels loved when we do this.

Assignment #1: Find out what makes your students tick.

Things to Consider:
> ➢ How well do you really know your students?
> ➢ Do you know specific things about each kid to get the most out of them?

Assignment #2: Be a safe place for someone.

Things to Consider:
> ➢ Manuel came to me because he saw me as a safe place, a place where he could be himself.
> ➢ Can you adjust your approach with someone to become their safe place at school?

Assignment #3: To love better you've got to know better.

Things to Consider:
> ➢ It's incredible how much greater our capacity is to love when we actually know the person we say we love.
> ➢ Be interested in your students and ask them questions.

Assignment #4: Be a student of your students.

Things to Consider:
> ➢ Take the time to consider each one of your kids.
> ➢ Intentionally think about 2-3 students each week and learn something about them.

Chapter 12
The Spiritual War Around You

"For we do not wrestle against flesh and blood, but against principalities, against powers, against the rulers of the darkness of this age, against spiritual hosts of wickedness in the heavenly places."
Ephesians 6:12 NKJV

I have a strong conviction that God placed me in the classroom for a certain time and a specific purpose. I realized during this time that He was giving me discernment to see beyond what I would typically see. There were numerous times that I would say just the right thing at just the right time that a student or group of students needed to hear. I knew it was the Lord because students would react with a look of astonishment on their faces and even approach me after class asking how I knew to mention a particular subject that day. I believe that when you stay close to the Lord, through Bible reading and prayer, He will provide you with insight that you ordinarily wouldn't have.

I became aware of this dynamic when I was interacting with a couple of girls named Sadie and Nicole. They were close friends. At certain times

I would go off course from the lesson plan and speak on subjects those girls really needed to hear. I would go on rants and get borderline "preachy" in the middle of my lessons. I would preach with a zeal that even surprised me. I remember, during one of my rants, delving into the importance of choosing who you date or befriend wisely. I talked about how important it is to observe how the person you're interested in treats others as a way of predicting how he's going to treat you. I couldn't let up on the subject. It was as if God was screaming truth toward somebody in that room like their life depended on it.

Later that day, the girls both thanked me for what I had to say, showing me how much they appreciated it. Over a few months they each won Morrissey Awards for different breakthroughs I noticed in class. I tried to display the week's awards on my door in the hallway so other students could see something positive about each winner. *Maybe they will congratulate each other in between classes,* I thought. I noticed the kids would hold their heads up a little higher when I would do this. It was the end of the week, and I was taking down the previous week's awards from the hallway door when Sadie stopped me. "Don't take mine down Mr. Morris," she pleaded. I was startled. *She really values this,* I thought. That's when I first noticed how much it meant to her.

You see, I was beginning to realize why I went on that rant a few months prior. Sadie tended to associate with, let's say, a questionable group. She gravitated toward boys that were heavily into the street culture, many of whom were in gangs. To me, it was a bit odd. By appearances, Sadie looked like the typical suburban white girl who wouldn't have anything in common with her friends. It wasn't until the weekend football game that I got a clear picture of how precarious her situation was. It was Friday night. I was leaning over the fences, rooting for our team when I spotted Sadie out of the corner of my eye. She was holding hands with a very familiar-looking student. It was Montrell Willis. Montrell was not to be trifled with. I had taught him when he was a freshman several years prior, and he only lasted a few weeks. He was a known gang member and hitman. Montrell was the kind of person who had no problem whatsoever walking into a building and shooting multiple people in the back of the head. It was a wonder he was permitted to walk the streets, let alone attend the local high school football game. Yet here he was, locking arms with Sadie from my third block class. I couldn't believe my eyes. I took several glances in their direction to make sure I saw things correctly.

I couldn't let it go. All night I kept thinking about what I had seen. "Is she crazy?" I yelled repeatedly. Of course, it wasn't long before I sensed the question in my mind, *Should I say something to her? It's not my business. But it is my business!* To say I was double-minded about it would be an understatement. I went back and forth in my mind about it all weekend before finally deciding to seek some advice on the subject. My sister, Christina, has always been a source of spiritual counsel and insight in my life. I figured I'd bounce my thoughts off her and get some advice. After a thorough description of the matter, my sister responded, "Christopher, she's in a burning building and disoriented from the smoke." Her analogy struck home for me. She went on to provide scientific research that detailed the effects of smoke inhalation from fire victims. It clouds your judgment and sense of reality. She told me how, especially if she's involved with this guy sexually, the soul tie is so strong she can't see things clearly whatsoever. She was adamant that I had to say something to her. Oh boy. Here we go!

After our phone call, I began thinking through how I could orchestrate an opportunity to confront Sadie about her relationship. I knew she had a degree of respect for me and would at least listen to what I had to say. Like many in her class, she struggled with the Algebra II curriculum. She needed tutoring badly, so I decided I'd use this as my opportunity. I asked Sadie and Nicole to stay after school for thirty minutes for a must-needed tutoring session. Everything was working out perfectly. The Lord made the opportunity perfectly obvious for me as Nicole had to leave tutoring early that afternoon, leaving Sadie and me alone in tutoring. After answering a few more math questions, I brought up my concern.

"I have to say it," I said. "Your boyfriend. What are you thinking?"

"What do you mean, Mr. Morris?" she replied.

"I know he's in a gang and I know his reputation. He's going to either be dead or in jail. Which one of those would you like to be?" Sadie stared at me, blank-faced. "You're in a burning building and suffering from smoke inhalation, so you're not thinking clearly. If he goes around in fits of anger and kills people without a second thought, how do you think he's going to treat you eventually?" I went on and on in a straightforward manner. She never got defensive or antagonistic. She merely listened as I said my piece. She even thanked me for speaking my mind and then left for the day. *Welp,* I thought. *This should be interesting.*

I decided to trust God with the results. I knew I couldn't control what would happen, but that I was only accountable for doing my part and saying what the Lord put in my heart to say. I went about my business for the next few days, teaching class and doing what I do. Sadie was amazingly quiet during that time. She didn't say a lot to me at all. Nicole, however, was another story. After class the next week, Nicole strolled over to my desk to talk. "I want you to know, Mr. Morris, that Sadie has been thinking a lot about what you had to say."

"Really?" I asked.

"Yes, she's giving it a lot of thought and seriously considering breaking up with him."

Oh Lord, please let it be so, I thought. I found out that a lot of Sadie's girlfriends had been telling her the same thing, that she needed to get away from him.

I watched closely for the next couple of weeks, and then one day Sadie herself told me that she had broken up with him. She seemed triumphant in the way she expressed it like she was proud of herself. I was ecstatic. "That's a relief to hear," I told her. "I'm proud of you."

"Yep, I couldn't stop thinking about what you said and knew I had to do it," she said. I was so encouraged and happy that I didn't know what to do with myself. The first thing I did that afternoon was tell my sister the good news. We both celebrated and thanked God for His deliverance. It's so funny looking back at how wondrous and amazing the Lord really is. He is doing profound and incredible works right around us every day, but if you're not looking for them, you'll miss them.

No one else at that school, to my knowledge, was even aware of the battle raging for Sadie's soul. The other teachers were going about their business, teaching their lessons, and focusing on their daily routines. They had no idea that a spiritual war was raging all around right next to them. Life and death were literally on the line. Over the next couple of months, I was about to see just how clear this reality was.

I'd like to say that Sadie had a clean break and never relapsed, but alas, this wasn't the case. A couple of weeks after she broke up with her boyfriend, I noticed she was acting a little aloof and distant from her classmates and me. I asked Nicole, and she soon informed me that Sadie was entertaining the idea of getting back together with him. In many ways, I couldn't believe it, but from my experience, I knew to expect this. There was nothing else I could do. It was out of my hands. I had done what the Lord asked me to do and said my piece. Now, the results were in His hands. I watched the situation as closely as I could over the next month or so before it happened.

It was over the Christmas break. I was wasting time on Facebook scrolling through my newsfeed when I saw what was hard to conceive. Montrell's face was plastered all over my screen by the local news station. Montrell had just shot three people, including a pregnant mother with a baby and was on the loose. The TBI (Tennessee Bureau of Investigation) had listed Montrell on its most-wanted list, and there was an all-out manhunt underway for his whereabouts. Man, was God on the front lines with this one or what? I quickly checked the comment section under the posted news story, and many students from my high school were telling people to check with Sadie, his girlfriend. What if she was going to be arrested for being an accomplice or sheltering him? Her life as she knew it would be over.

My mind was racing. Did Sadie ever call it quits with him for good? Was she in trouble? I couldn't believe how quickly the realities of God's warning had come to pass. I immediately shared the story with my sister, showing her the news story link. We marveled together at the Lord's perfect timing and stood in awe of the sheer magnitude of the situation. It was a stark reminder that when the Lord puts it in your heart to speak up or do something, you do it. Don't hesitate. You are literally the difference between life and death for someone. The story made headlines, and the rumors were buzzing. A lot of the girls in class were saying that she had gotten back together with him and that they had warned her over and over to get away from Montrell.

As for Sadie, she was nowhere to be found. She had transferred to another high school over Christmas break and had mostly withdrawn from her peers. There were plenty of rumors to go around, but very few people had any real concrete information. The situation was in the Lord's hands now. I went about my business for another week or so before someone familiar visited me. It was Sadie's mom. I had met her before at our various parent-teacher conferences, but this visit was different. She had a look in her eyes like she couldn't wait to talk. I invited her to have a seat, and she began.

"I cannot begin to thank you enough for what you said to my daughter and how you've treated her this year. Sadie goes on and on about how much she respects you, and I couldn't be more thankful." I was floored and amazed at what I was hearing. She went on to tell me how she had tried over and over for months to get Sadie to break up with Montrell, but it was as if her words would fall on deaf ears. "After she spoke with you, she began seriously considering breaking up with him for the first time," she continued. "Thank God they were on a break at the time it happened. I believe this was the wake-up call she needed for a long time." She went on and on about the nuances of the situation and mentioned how she had been praying over this situation and her daughter's life continually. It was a little strange to me that the mother didn't seem to have more authority over her daughter's decisions, but I committed just to listen and only speak when and what I felt the Lord wanted me to.

She opened up a great deal with me over that hour-long conversation, but by the end, it was clear that the Lord had used me strategically amid a raging spiritual battle over Sadie's life. It's astonishing to see how casual and blinded most people are to the war raging around them. For many of these students, it was as if they were walking in the middle of the crossfire, clueless to the bullets flying by their heads. Even when speaking with Sadie, it felt as if she wasn't entirely there. Sure, her body was in the room, but her mind was somewhere floating in the clouds. It was like she lacked even the most rudimentary reasoning skills needed to apply life-saving action in her life.

I left the conversation feeling that both Sadie's mother and I had committed the situation to the Lord. We had seen God snatch Sadie from the jaws of death and had confidence in Him to finish the work. Wow, Lord! The things you want to do through your people is quite the adventure. Life and death are on the line. You want us to play our part that you destined for us from the foundation of the world. Eventually, we'll develop new relationships and get to know you more in the process.

Assignment #1: Sometimes, you need to say something!

Things to Consider:
> ➤ I can only imagine what may have come of Sadie if I didn't take the risk to speak to her about her relationship.
> ➤ You don't know how close your students may be to the brink of death. You may be their last line of defense from calamity.
> ➤ Are you going to have the courage to speak your heart? They may not act like it in the moment, but they're listening to you.

Assignment #2: Be aware of the war!

Things to Consider:
> ➤ Are you aware of the spiritual war around you?
> ➤ There's more going on than meets the eye.
> ➤ Ask God to help you play your part.

Chapter 13
The Problem Outlined

"I wouldn't wish any specific thing for any specific person — it's none of my business. But the idea that a four-year degree is the only path to worthwhile knowledge is insane. It's insane."
Mike Rowe

It seemed that every day, there were news stories detailing the hunt for Montrell. Police finally found him at an apartment, and the trial scheduled soon after. It's an amazing thing to watch the eerie reality of gang culture played out in the courtroom. Several key witnesses were petrified to say what they knew in fear of backlash from Montrell's gang affiliates. Their concern was for a good reason. At least one or two witnesses' houses were shot up after testifying in court. If you followed the news reports on Facebook, you could see comments from suspicious people warning the witnesses to keep their mouths shut. I can't imagine what it must feel like to grow up with that culture all around you. Everyday things we take for granted, like walking around in the neighborhood, aren't options for many in these gang-riddled communities. You even must be careful about what color clothes you wear. I remember asking one of my students that year some probing questions about gang culture. His response? "You gotta keep your head down."

So sad! I stared at him in disbelief. Not only was this news heartbreaking, but I was equally astounded at how casual and common this sort of life seemed for my kids. Having to keep your head down was a natural part of life for them. This shouldn't be! And the sad part of it all was, it wasn't necessarily their fault. For most of them, they were born into it. The student I spoke with was a third-generation Blood. The only reason many of these kids had food to eat was because of the money provided to them from the selling of drugs. Once you accept payment, you are expected to be available when called upon. It's a vicious cycle.

Equally amazing to me is the reality that our educational system doesn't adapt accountability measures for schools whose communities encompass these sorts of realities. Why are those teachers held to the same criteria as teachers who are in more affluent areas and don't have to worry about these kinds of challenges? There's no way that a student is going to be able to concentrate on his studies or perform on a standardized test if he is having to worry about bullets flying by his head or where his next meal is going to come from. It's reasonable to have an entirely different expectation for schools that serve more affluent communities with solid family structures and the sense of safety. Kids who are living with constant chaos all around them don't care about or prioritize the same things that affluent kids do. Think of it as Maslow's hierarchy of needs. You must have food, water, shelter, and an underlying sense of security and love. Then all the other things can be addressed. When you're missing the aforementioned, other important aspects such as grades and test scores take a back seat.

We need to take a harder look at the needs of the communities that these schools serve and tailor our systems and processes to do best by those students. Why are we forcing all these kids to go to a four-year university, taking on massive amounts of debt, when we know that they aren't going to stick with the program? Especially when there are so many great and viable options at community colleges and trade schools that cost less money, take less time, and, in many cases, lead to higher-paying jobs. It seems to me that four-year universities and colleges have all the leverage and they know it. Therefore, they continue to raise tuition year after year. They know that the high schools are going to continue to funnel kids, whether they're prepared for it or not, to their universities, and that the banks are going to give them an unlimited amount of loan money that the colleges can profit from. Why wouldn't they continue to raise tuition? If colleges know there's virtually no limit to how much money students can get to pay them, they're going to continue to increase tuition costs. There's more money to be had, and they are going to take full advantage of it. That's just smart business.

Conversely, if we guided students in the direction that best suits them and how they're wired, colleges would be forced to compete, therefore lowering tuition costs in the process. Furthermore, students would actually have a shot at making it with the hope for a brighter future. And don't get me started on student loans. It may be the primary culprit. In any other loan agreement made in America, you must provide proof of income before a loan is disbursed. This is true for a mortgage or a car loan. But with college loans, an eighteen-year-old kid can be issued an unlimited amount of money, regardless of the prospect that their chosen major will yield any ability to pay that loan back. It's madness. No one should be allowed to borrow $100,000 to get a degree in music theory, but it happens every day. These kinds of realities are destroying this next generation, and it needs to stop.

When my father graduated from medical school back in the 70s, he graduated with less than $40,000 in school loans. It was manageable because he had the income of a doctor and was able to balance his debt and living expenses. Today, the average medical student graduates with approximately $167,000 in medical school debt. Couple that with $37,000 in average college debt in the U.S. and you're looking at $204,000 in student loans upon graduation. Yikes!

It took my father nearly twelve years to pay off the $40,000 with a doctor's income. How in the world does one pay off a debt of over $200,000? That's virtually your entire life. It's at least the equivalent of a 30-year mortgage. We've got to do things differently and put pressure on institutions to be more competitive. That doesn't happen until we realize that there are other options available to our students other than the four-year university experience. It doesn't happen until we wake up and truly educate students as to the repercussions of their choices and promote the idea to think for themselves. We need to look at where those choices lead and weigh the consequences.

I think many of our students completely lack the ability to reason through these kinds of implications. Just look at Sadie. As I said earlier, she seemed to lack the most rudimentary of reasoning skills necessary to apply life-saving action in her life. I'm convinced something wasn't functioning correctly upstairs. I don't mean that in a mean or incendiary way. I'm merely saying that many of our students are lacking the ability to process information correctly. Curt Thompson, in his bestseller *The Soul of Shame* presents compelling evidence of the adverse effects of shame and its role on the mind's ability to reason and exercise sound judgment. There's significant evidence to suggest shame's impact on the neocortex which is largely responsible for reasoning, judgment, and decision-making. In other words, the very presence of shame in someone's life could shut down the proper function of the neocortex in the brain, thus crippling that person's ability to logically think things through.

I believe this is a huge reason why the Morrissey Awards were having such a positive effect on my students, and why recognition of this sort needs to be in every classroom in the country. Instead of shaming students, the character awards lift their spirits, giving them a jolt of freedom to feel comfortable with themselves. It removes shame and thus has the potential to counteract the adverse effects on the neocortex. I think everyone can agree that our upcoming generation could stand to improve in the areas of reasoning, judgment, and decision-making. Let's tackle this issue at the source of the problem. We must dig deeper and intrinsically impact each one of our students.

I once had an interesting conversation with a friend of mine, a former teacher. He told me how he once taught a teenage girl who saw absolutely no problem with having multiple babies in high school. She had no job, wasn't married, and had no plans for either. I suppose she planned to get money from the government and live off that. He tried to talk through the implications of that decision with her but could never make any headway. He went through the practicalities of getting through high school and getting married first before having a baby. He walked her through the income projections of people who chose that path versus the one she planned to make for herself. He logically tried to walk her through all the different scenarios but to no avail. She couldn't track with him and seemed, as he described it, to not have the ability to reason.

This is why a tactic to penetrate these kinds of moments is what our country and communities need the most. Perhaps shame was playing a role in this young girl's life. Maybe it was affecting the neocortex of her brain and hindering her ability to reason and make beneficial decisions for her life and the lives of her future children. Maybe she was belittled continuously and shamed at home. If we could begin to identify the source and curb its stronghold in the minds of our youth, we could begin to heal America! Let's breathe life into these kids. The Morrissey Character Awards are a great way to start. I'm convinced, and many others are too! People don't need reminders of what's wrong with them. They already know! Their shame is screaming their faults at them every moment of the day. When you completely ignore the obvious and communicate something good and of value to them in ways like this, it frees the soul. It enables the mind to think clearly and provides hope.

> When you completely ignore the obvious and communicate something good and of value to them in ways like this, it frees the soul. It enables the mind to think clearly and provides hope.

It also opens the door to relationship, which is perhaps the most valuable component to it all. I once heard a wise person say, "One relationship can make all the difference in the world." It may sound cliché, but isn't it the truth? Some of you have had an excellent job for twenty-five or more years simply because of a healthy trusting relationship with your boss. My mother is an excellent example. She grew up with little income and no biological father in the home. She often dreamed of the day she could get out of her household and run towards a better life. Her one relationship with her husband and my father has provided her an extraordinarily prosperous and comfortable life in adulthood. I don't think she's had to work in nearly forty years! In scripture, Joseph benefited greatly from relationship. Even though he had a rough start, just one strong relationship with Pharaoh made Joseph the second most powerful man in the world by the time he was thirty.

So many of our youth don't have healthy relationships and honestly, don't possess the necessary character traits or habits even to form them. As educators, we must stand in the gap. We must build a bridge to a real, mutually beneficial relationship with them for their sake and the nation's. If you don't open the door to relationship, students will never open up to you. If they don't open up to you, they'll never listen to what you have to say. If they don't listen to what you have to say, and your words don't carry weight with them, you're not educating anyone. You're wasting your time.

I suppose it boils down, once again, to our pride as people and our incessant ability to think more highly of ourselves than we ought. For the life of me, I can't understand why I ever thought I could march into a school like that and just expect the students to respect me. Like an idiot, I once started the school year off by listing my degrees and academic accomplishments as evidence for why the kids should respect me. Suffice it to say; it didn't work. I might have made matters worse. It was as if I made a personal challenge to each knucklehead in the class to make my life a living hell and personally show me why they didn't respect me. They couldn't care less about my degrees or grade point average. I had to earn their respect personally.

It is the lesson all teachers must learn, hopefully, sooner rather than later. You must earn their respect. So, I'll leave you with this question. **What are you going to do to earn the right to speak into your kid's lives?** There must be some action on your part that demonstrates love and care to each one of them personally. If there isn't, don't expect their respect. Don't expect much for that matter, especially if you work in a challenging environment. Have something you continue to do intentionally that demonstrates your love and care for your students. If you're like me, just the act of doing something loving and on purpose begins to change your heart toward your kids. Talk is cheap! Your actions speak volumes.

Assignment #1: Don't ignore the shame!

Things to Consider:
> ➤ Shame has debilitating effects on your students and their ability to process information.
> ➤ Why do we continue to ignore this issue?
> ➤ Affirming your students' value is critical to disarming the power of shame.

Assignment #2: Guide students toward their best option.

Things to Consider:
> ➤ Community colleges are increasingly becoming better options for students as the market demands specific skillsets.
> ➤ Many bachelor's degrees hold little to no value in the marketplace.

Assignment #3: Know your students well enough to guide them where they'll thrive.

Things to Consider:
> ➤ If your students' families can't afford it and your students haven't shown any ability to thrive in the traditional 4-year university experience, don't guide them to that direction!
> ➤ Community colleges cost less money, take less time, and often lead to higher-paying jobs because job placement is their focus.
> ➤ Maybe they need to get a job and go straight to work.
> ➤ Know your students well enough to know where they'll thrive best.

Chapter 14
The System Restructured

*"Education is not the learning of facts, but the
training of the mind to think."*
Albert Einstein

Our educational system needs to address several areas immediately for the sake of this generation. We can't afford to act like the status quo is ok while so much is at stake!

The failure is not an option mindset

Our students need to learn to become accountable. They need to see where their choices lead and learn to take corrective action where necessary. Right now, the educational environment is not allowing kids to feel the weight of their decisions or get an honest look at where they stand. Just recently, a teacher in Florida was fired for refusing to give her students credit for work that they never turned in. Apparently, school policy requires all students to receive a minimum of 50% credit even for work that was never completed. What kind of policy is that? In what world are you given anything for nothing, let alone 50% credit? We're creating a false sense of reality for this generation that in no way reflects real life.

I remember the intense pressure I was continually under in my time in the classroom to inflate grades and pass failing students. I believe the reason for this pressure was 3-fold:

- Graduation rate requirements
- English as a second language (ESL) law
- Special Education Requirements

1. Graduation Rates

It all boils down to funding. In my district and many others throughout the nation, schools lose funding if they don't maintain specific graduation rates each year. It creates all sorts of problems and increases the likelihood of unethical behavior. If a student who has practically done nothing the entire school year is failing in the 40s or 50s, the administration often puts extreme pressure on the teacher to get them to at least a 60% average. If the student has at least a 60% average, they're eligible for a computer-based program called credit recovery. Credit recovery is a module-based software program that students take after school for months and if completed, can have their 60% average changed to a 70% average and therefore pass the class they previously failed.

2. English as a second language (ESL)

The English as a second language or ESL issue is a different matter entirely. In my state, it is illegal to fail a student deemed an English language learner if the reason for failure is due to a language barrier. The problem here is that it's practically impossible to prove why a student did or did not fail a class due to a language barrier. From a teacher's perspective, there's no way they are going to fail an ESL student for fear that they will be accused of breaking the law. Many of the ESL students speak little English, and it is hard to tell if they don't understand something due to language barriers or basic comprehension. It's insane. How can a law that a student can't fail exist? This sort of legislation distorts a young person's sense of reality and is inconsistent with the real world. If I fail to pay my mortgage, there isn't a law that keeps the bank from repossessing my house or other belongings. You either know the information, or you don't. You either have an education, or you don't. It doesn't matter what the piece of paper says you receive on graduation day. In reality, we're just lying to the kids, saying we've given them an education when we have not.

3. Special Education Requirements

There's a similar gray area in the realm of special education. A student who's been diagnosed with a learning disability has all kinds of leverage over the classroom teacher. Their teacher is given a laundry list of "accommodations" that he or she is supposed to make for every diagnosed student. These accommodations are lengthy, vague, and impractical in many cases. I'm convinced that any student with a good enough lawyer can win a lawsuit against his or her teacher that they didn't accommodate adequately in class. It happens all the time. A teacher must provide individual time, extended opportunities to turn in late work, extra time on tests and quizzes, and a host of 15 or more specific accommodations all while eyeing 30 other students who have specific needs at the same time. It's impossible to do every accommodation on any given day. If teachers are brave enough to fail one of these special education students, they better have extensive paperwork lined up proving they didn't slip up on any one of these accommodations. Otherwise, they've set themselves up for a nice lawsuit or, even worse, the loss of their job. I've known many educators who refuse to fail special education or ESL students, and I can't say I blame them. The system forces them to if they want to keep their jobs. It forces teachers to set the kids up to fail at life because we can't fail them now when it's safe to do so.

Standardized Testing

In my opinion, standardized testing in our schools has gotten entirely out of control. It's more about big money from testing and textbook companies than trying to adequately measure and assist grade school students. There are some reports that in grades 3 through 8, some schools are giving at least ten standardized tests a year, pulling students out of class repeatedly and decreasing the amount of much-needed learning time in the classroom. That's not even including the class time taken away to devote for test prep for each one of these corporate money-making tests. I once heard a compelling analogy regarding standardized testing that involved something as simple as a ruler. He made the case that a test is simply a tool. It's a tool used to measure results. But it's important to realize that a tool is only useful for measuring certain things. It's not useful for measuring all things nor appropriate for all situations. While a standard 6-inch ruler helps measure the length of linear objects, you'd have to agree that it does not help measure the circumference of a basketball. It's not pliable nor has the right shape. Likewise, you wouldn't use a ruler to measure the temperature of the weather outside. It's not the right tool for the given situation. What if someone expected you to measure your weight in-lbs and handed you a ruler to get the results? That wouldn't make much sense either. In much the same way, the American educational system uses standardized tests to measure all situations in our public schools and, I would argue, is using the wrong tool to do so.

For example, when I first began my teaching career, the district was heavily stressing a concept referred to as backward design as a best practice for teaching students. Instead of directly teaching the many state standards throughout the year, we were stressed to provide students an expansive word problem that encompassed all the skills they would need to acquire throughout a given unit. Teachers were expected to act more as coaches or referees and facilitate students' self-discovery of the various standards in an algebra curriculum. In other words, we couldn't simply show our students the "wheel" and how it works. We had to present them with a series of problems and hope they literally reinvent the "wheel" in our class time together. This was an exhausting process. It had some merit but was impractical in that it allowed students to explore a subject in a deep way but never afforded enough time to cover all the material the district required us to cover. They wanted us to go a mile wide and a mile deep at the same time. This is simply not possible. It's one or the other. If the district truly wanted us to take our time and go deep into the subject at hand, they should have dramatically reduced the number of standards we were required to cover throughout the year. Instead, they forced us to teach in this way but would become irate when we couldn't cover the many standards they wanted to be taught by the end of a given quarter. The

The System Restructured

standardized test would serve much like the ruler in that it was designed to assess many standards when our students had only covered a fraction of those standards because of the required teaching methods.

Why couldn't schools create custom assessments that tested the learning that took place over the course of the school year? This would be a far more accurate measure of what students truly learned throughout a school year. Instead, we have teachers slowly moving through the standards because of the required teaching methods and then scrambling a few weeks before the standardized test to directly teach specific standards that could have been taught in the first place if they were just left alone. I recently read an article of a coalition of 19 or so Georgia public schools who are petitioning their state department of education to do just that. They are trying to get off the state-mandated standards and administer their own school-site assessments. The people have had enough and are ready to take ownership of the education of their residents. We can't keep letting big money corporations profit at our expense and the expense of our children.

As an educational system, we need to completely restructure. All the systems, assessments, and goals need to be realigned around a different paradigm. It should be about building students up and getting the most out of each child individually. Suddenly, instead of having some linear benchmark everyone must reach, the aim could be completely different. Why not use assessments as a tool rather than the goal in and of itself? Why is success seen as a test score rather than seen as helping a student find and develop their strengths? We need to strive to get the most out of our students and stop asking kids to give us what they don't have. Instead, let's look at where they are and the gifts and talents they possess and do everything in our power to maximize what they have and who they are. Assessments should be used to inform the educator where the student stands so he or she can adjust and better guide the student. Let's design a system that allows every child to become a better version of themselves instead of trying to force them to be something that they're not. This is the solution that the Morrissey Character Awards and Model can provide.

In one sense, they practically provide something that education desperately needs in order to improve results: leverage. Schools don't have any leverage in the eyes of their students. By leverage, I mean they don't have something they present before students that students value so much that they're willing to work harder than ever to get what the schools offer. The recognition and identity these awards can offer students will not only be desired, they will be craved. Students are desperate for affirmation from anyone that they indeed matter and that who they are matters. Being kids, they are desperate for attention from their peers and this process hits both birds with one stone. The problem is, society at large has no clue how badly young people crave affirmation. They don't realize that students want it so badly that they would be willing to make great concessions in order to receive it. And this leads us to the truth about life that education refuses to acknowledge.

You get out of life what you have the leverage to negotiate. You wonder why kids are so lazy and unmotivated to put forth even the slightest bit of effort? It's because schools haven't presented something before them that they value so much that they're willing to pay the price in order to get it. Michael Jordan doesn't have to try very hard to have young people lining up and forking over hundreds of dollars on his latest shoes. The kids already crave what he offers and go through great lengths in order to get it. Apple doesn't have to pull teeth to get people to fork over thousands of dollars on their latest iPhones. In some cases, people will line up and even sleep outside of the store in anticipation of their latest offering. You see, the more a customer values what it is that they are being offered, the more a company can expect to get out of them in order to receive it. The same is true in education. You need to offer something before the eyes of your students that they desperately desire. If you do, they'll work for you with their blood, sweat, and tears.

> You need to offer something before the eyes of your students that they desperately desire. If you do, they'll work for you with their blood, sweat, and tears.

Do you remember Wyatt from the school-wide Valley Award dance? He was, to put it delicately... a piece of work. I had just incorporated my character awards all year long and the classes were responding well to them. By the end of the year, nearly every student had won at least one

The System Restructured

award except one young man... Wyatt. Wyatt was a creative type and hated math class with every facet of his being. He was sarcastic, rude, and completely incorrigible the entire year. I looked extremely hard for even one positive thing I could recognize him for that year and couldn't think of a thing. In his eyes, I represented the devil for forcing him to do math. It brought out the absolute worst in him. To make matters even worse, he didn't even seem to care one iota about my character awards. He simply brushed me off day after day.

It wasn't until the very last day of that school year that Wyatt made his true feelings known. "How come I was the only one in the class who never got an award?" Wyatt yelled violently. His question took me off guard. I didn't even know he cared. After gathering my thoughts, I responded. "Okay Wyatt, name one positive thing you did this year that was worthy of acknowledgment." The silence was deafening. Nearly a minute went by and Wyatt couldn't answer my question. "There you go," I said. All my students knew you couldn't just act the same way you always acted and be entitled to an award. You had to do something positive and different that you wouldn't normally do to show personal growth if you wanted to be acknowledged. I told him that maybe he could win one next year if I heard anything positive about his decisions from his other teachers. Wyatt left my class with a look of anger but also with an expression of "guilty as charged" written on his face.

As the Lord would have it, that wasn't the end of my journey with Wyatt. The following year brought with it more opportunities to expand the awards school-wide. During these school-wide character award ceremonies, it became my practice to add flash-mob dance choreography with the students in order to amp up the event and make the awards more meaningful. It dawned on me one day that this could be my opportunity to patch things up with Wyatt since he was bummed about never winning a Morrissey Award and being so poorly behaved in my math class the previous year. Wyatt was deeply creative and loved song and dance. He was also very funny, and I knew he could make the school-wide award dance-off fun for the student body. I reached out to him about helping me coordinate the routine and he jumped at the chance. This is where we were able to cultivate a healthy relationship. It was during these after-school dance routines that Wyatt was able to see that I wasn't the devil he had always perceived me to be. We learned to enjoy each other's company and he really did make the awards fun for everyone. I decided it was time to finally give Wyatt the much-awaited Morrissey Award he had been waiting for over a year to receive.

I went straight to work. I knew I wanted to call Wyatt's award the "Fearless" Morrissey Award. I gave him the award for being a tone-setter and not an imitator! For every award I made, I always left a detailed reason for winning that was personal to the winner. It said, "Every time I call on you to put yourself out there for the school, you step up without a moment's hesitation. That's fearless! It's also an endearing quality about you that's much needed in this world. Wyatt, thanks for being you!" Along with his award, I used the donation money from the non-profit to get him a $50 gift card. The gift card was for an outlet store in order to get some new clothes that he desperately needed. I was really looking forward to giving him the gift card because he had literally gone through hell that year, losing his home to mold and was even homeless during much of the school year.

I called him to my room and had the students in my class applauding him when he entered the room in order to make him feel special. It was awesome. He smiled from ear to ear and thanked me from the heart, but not before bowing before his peers and soaking the moment in. Later that afternoon, Wyatt came and found me before leaving for the day. It was at this time that I heard the most genuine and mind-blowing statement regarding this process I ever heard a student say. "Mr. Morris," Wyatt said. "Don't get me wrong. I really appreciate the 50-dollar gift card to get new clothes. I really need it right now. But that Morrissey Award means 100 times more to me than that gift card ever will." *Really?* I thought. That's amazing. A simple certificate, a piece of paper with words of affirmation on it meant that much to him. It was profound to consider. But the truth was laid out right before me.

These kids are starving for affirmation. They may have full minds, but their souls are empty. For some, it's even a matter of life or death. One definition for affirmation says, "to give (life) a heightened sense of value, typically through the experience of something emotionally or spiritually uplifting." Why would we, as educators, not seek to heighten our students' sense of value through an experience of emotional or spiritual uplifting? If students value themselves more highly, they'll be able to communicate their value more clearly to others. If they can communicate their value more clearly to others, they'll be able to offer more value to the world. When people are viewed as valuable, they can demand more compensation, dictate the terms of contractual arrangements, and carve out a better future for themselves. Hello?!?! The more valuable you are to a company, the more compensation you can expect to be paid. The more value your skills or products have in the eyes of customers, the more you can charge for those skills or products. I don't care how much education a person attains, if they don't see themselves as valuable, it's going to be very hard for that person to convince others of their value. And if they can't do that… they can't expect higher pay. If we really want education to provide opportunities for our children and be a gateway toward prosperity, you must affirm them and give them a heightened sense of value. I don't care how they act or what they say… all students want to become a better version of themselves and want to see their value work for them in this world. It's our job to support that.

Assignment #1: Let your students fail.

Things to Consider:
> ➢ Why? It's good for them. How else will students learn what it takes to be successful?
> ➢ Give them a chance to learn what doesn't work so they can head in the right direction.

Assignment #2: We've got to do less things but do them well. (Quality over Quantity)

Things to Consider:
> ➢ Our teachers and students would be much better off if we concentrated on doing less things well.
> ➢ Let's pick a few tasks and do them well with excellence. Instead, what we have right now is a system that forces educators to do too many things at once therefore yielding minimal results with lower quality.
> ➢ I've never searched for an average plumber or handyman. I want people who are the very best at doing the one service I need performed.
> ➢ People spend money on individuals who do one thing well.
> ➢ Why do we handle students as if they need to do everything while never mastering anything?

Assignment #3: Use assessments differently.

Things to Consider:
> ➢ Our society has gotten the purpose of assessments completely backwards.
> ➢ Assessments should be used to inform the teacher, not label the child.
> ➢ The goal should be to discover who a child is and where his or her strengths truly lie. It should inform both the teacher and the student whether they know the material without shaming them or making the child feel stupid.
> ➢ Assessments should be seen purely as a tool to help the teacher know how to teach each child, not as the goal in and of itself.

The System Restructured

➢ What if the goal of education was to hear a student tell you what they had learned instead of hearing them ask, "What was my score?"

Chapter 15
The Solution

"Value is not determined by those who set the price. Value is determined by those who choose to pay it."
Simon Sinek

"You get out of life what you have the leverage to negotiate." I once heard that quote from former NBA player and current ESPN sports broadcaster, Jalen Rose. He was discussing the latest multimillion-dollar contract deal secured by a prominent athlete. His statement struck me. It had a ring of truth to it that I had never fully considered. "He's right," I thought. Leverage is the reason a high school baseball player with no education can sign the dotted line and receive a signing bonus in excess of 2 million dollars. With the stroke of a pen, he's an instant millionaire. It's because of a simple fact of life. You're worth what someone is willing to pay. Someone out there can make hundreds of millions if they can secure a talent that can throw a 95mph fastball. To a person like this, 2 million is nothing and worth the money. It also got me to thinking about the various things that people are willing to pay big bucks for. My wife will easily spend $70 on her makeup, but I would never spend a penny on it. Why? Because to her, it's worth it. Just because I personally don't value what she values doesn't make the price of makeup any less valuable in the marketplace. You're worth what SOMEONE is willing to pay. SOMEONE!!! Not everyone. Suddenly, I realized the problem that the educational community was facing and what the Lord was allowing me to discover. The educational community doesn't have leverage with students. They don't offer anything students want so desperately that they're willing to pay the price, so to speak, in order to get it. If education had something like this to offer students, kids would be bending over backward, giving their blood, sweat, and tears in the classroom to get this offering.

> You're worth what SOMEONE is willing to pay. SOMEONE!!! Not everyone.

This is where the Morrissey Character Awards can fill this void. The one thing I was able to discover is just how badly these kids want these things. They want them badly for deep and personal reasons. For one, they practically offer the one thing school-age kids want the most, recognition and attention from their peers. Think about it. Students will do just about anything to get attention from one another throughout a given school day. They'll interrupt teachers and make smart remarks... all to get a laugh. Many kids will act out and misbehave simply because it provides attention their way. This recognition process provides the attention they all crave so badly, but in a constructive way. Secondly, the awards offer affirmation. They are designed in a way that builds students up without shaming them, lowering their defenses. It speaks life into their very souls and brings life back out of them. When you're affirmed, you feel validated and more confident regarding the best aspects of yourself. It empowers you to try things, make mistakes, and learn. Lastly, the awards provide aspiration. They offer what I've heard called an aspirational identity. An aspirational identity is best described as "the opportunity to become a better version of yourself." For example, when a student wins the "Maturity" Morrissey Award for Outstanding Display of Personal Growth, they begin to see themselves as a mature person. The award reminds them that they can make mature decisions and they start to see themselves that way. There's a big difference between doing the right thing to get something out of it versus doing the right thing because you see yourself as a responsible, mature, or kind person.

Many students long to see themselves a certain way and therefore attribute more value to the awards if the award labels them by a characteristic they desperately want to personify. Aspirational identity is used in marketing departments for companies all around the world. Ford truck uses the slogan "Built Ford Tough" in their campaigns. The idea is to send a subliminal message to potential buyers that they will be a tough guy if they buy their trucks. Air Jordan sells an "I'm the man" identity with its shoe line that increases their value 5-fold. The same factor is true with the character award concept. Provide the opportunity to become a better version of yourself and your students will attribute more value to your awards. The more value your students attribute, the more leverage you have. The more leverage you have, the more you'll get out of your students.

Simon Sinek, world-renowned speaker and author of the best-seller, "Start with Why," makes a compelling case for the biology of the human brain and its effect on behavior. In his book, he details the differences between the limbic section of the brain (inner brain) and the neocortex section (outer brain). His research is fascinating in that it reveals that the outer layer, the neocortex, is mainly responsible for judgment, decision-making, reasoning, and all language. The interesting fact, however, is that this section has almost no effect on human behavior. It's the reason why people can be given all the facts and figures as to why they should make a certain decision, but in the end they won't because they often say, "it just doesn't feel right."

Conversely, the limbic or inner layer is responsible for all feelings or gut-level decisions. It's the section that responds to music and emotion and, here's the kicker; it has zero capacity for language. It has no capacity for language but is the same area that drives human behavior. The question begs, if this is true, does anyone see a problem about the primary way education is communicating with today's students? I would argue that education almost solely communicates with the neocortex, the part of the brain that has zero capacity for behavior change. THIS is a problem.

How can we continue to proclaim that education is the door to opportunity and ignore the scientifically-backed research that suggests our communication tactic doesn't alter human behavior? Education must begin to speak to the limbic area of students' brains. This is another reason why students respond so well to the character awards. The awards inspire and include music embedded in the presentation. They immediately tap into the limbic section of students' minds. Students are emotionally and intrinsically stirred, which opens their desire and capacity to alter their behavior. It's a no brainer. We need to act and communicate to the limbic brain first. Then the neocortex can be addressed. We must take this direction. Our nation's future is at stake.

Another component that the awards address is a demonstration of care. Each time a teacher takes the time to make one of these awards, it communicates to the student that their teacher thinks of them and cares for them personally. It's something I call a personal transaction of care. A personal transaction of care is a loving action toward someone that qualifies you to speak into their life. It provides a sense of goodwill between two individuals and creates the opportunity for relationship. It's a lot like banking. Imagine for a moment that you were a millionaire. Say you had a million dollars cash in the bank with a specific financial institution. You decide to take your family to a fun day at a carnival and need some cash on hand for the attractions. On your way to the event, you decide to drop by a bank that isn't yours on your way to the carnival. You pull up to the teller and ask for a crisp one-hundred-dollar bill. Do you know what that teller would say if you asked for your money? "I'm sorry, but you can't make a withdrawal from an account in which you haven't first made a deposit."

> A personal transaction of care is a loving action toward someone that qualifies you to speak into their life.

Now any person with a lick of sense knows you must have an account to make a withdrawal, but we don't apply this truth with people. If you expect to make a withdrawal from students, if you plan to get anything out of them, you must first put a deposit in them. You must have made a personal transaction of care. Once you've done that, they'll have something to give you when you make a withdrawal, and it will have earned interest!

They will respond with more than you put in them in the first place and it will blow your mind! And the best part of it all is that it's a blast! Life surrounded by those you've made personal transactions of care with is a joy. When people want to please you, it makes all the difference. It can be a reality for every teacher in the country. It boils down to a choice. Are you going to choose to make a personal transaction of care with your students each week? I hope you do. Your impact will be felt for the rest of your students' lives, and it will impact generations.

Morrissey Character Awards Accomplish 3 Primary Things:

1. Speak to the limbic section of students' brains, the part responsible for behavior.
2. Provide an aspirational identity with our awards that increases their value in the eyes of students. This increases the leverage a teacher has to influence student outcomes.
3. Demonstrate a personal transaction of care with each student. Remember, you can't make a withdrawal from an account in which you haven't first made a deposit!

The Loving Thing to Do

What's the loving thing to do? It's a simple question, but perhaps the most essential. It's the one question we should be asking when imagining how a new educational system might look. If our policies, practices, and actions don't correctly answer this simple question then what exactly are we doing? Is the decision we're about to make the loving thing to do for our students and teachers or not? If not, then it's the wrong action to take and the wrong protocol to implement. For example, is it loving to move principals around to different schools every year or two within a school system? I would argue not! But it happens in school systems throughout the nation each year. Just when teachers and students are starting to grasp the direction of the principal in charge, they must relearn everything all over again when the district reassigns their principal the following year as if he or she was a piece on a checkerboard.

In schools, the principal king. He or she has the power to set the direction and priorities of the school, and everyone else must fall in line.

Imagine you're trying to catch a ride to the beach for your summer vacation in Florida. The driver of your vehicle gets switched out every 2 hours. Let's say the first driver thinks the best way to get to Florida is to head south. You've headed that direction for a couple hours when suddenly your driver is replaced by another who thinks that Florida is in the northern direction. After another couple hours that driver is replaced with a person who thinks we need to head west. After two more hours, that driver is again replaced with someone who thinks northeast is the way to go. After 8 hours of travel, you're no closer to Florida than when you initially left. How would you feel? Perhaps frustrated? Tired? Confused and a bit hopeless? I think you get the point. That's exactly how it feels for teachers and students when the head decision-maker is replaced every 2 to 3 years. School goals change, priorities are redefined, and the direction of the school isn't given a chance to ride long enough for any real results to be seen or evaluated. It's not a loving thing to do.

Another example would be high stakes standardized testing. It isn't loving to both students and teachers alike. So much class time is taken away just to prepare for these tests much of which have nothing to do with the learning that took place over the school year. I've personally witnessed the devastating effect these big-money state assessments have on students. I believe it's abusive. I watched as my students were taken out of class to flood computer labs to prepare for these multiple-week long mandated tests. They lost nearly eight weeks of class time only to watch as the computer-based tests crashed, and the district decided not to count the results of the tests after all. Students were and are being robbed of the opportunity to learn. And if students aren't learning, then what's the point? Teachers are forced to cram facts down their students' throats in hopes that they might vomit it up on a test soon after. I once heard this practice described not as real education, but more like educational bulimia. Trust me. The students won't remember any of these facts 24 hours after they finish these exams.

Conversely, what if we allowed actual learning to take place? What if we taught kids how to think, how to ask good questions and follow their conclusions? Only then, would we be loving our students and setting them up for success. We must set a vision before the eyes of each student of the best version of themselves that they can be. It will give them hope and the ability to run towards what's possible for them with a grace upon their lives. Let's tear down the idea that the status quo is okay. It's not. Not even close! Let's remove everything that hinders and allow our students to breathe again. I want to give them air! I bet you do too. Let's revive the educational landscape and do what's loving!

About the Author

Christopher Morris is a speaker, author, and educational consultant from Chattanooga, TN. He and his beautiful wife, Hannah, work together in their company, Morrissey Model, and spread their unique message of how God's love and His ways are the only true answers to transforming the educational landscape across America. Christopher has 7 years' experience as a high school math teacher in a very diverse and economically disadvantaged school setting. His comedic storytelling and passion help paint an accurate picture of today's educational landscape and identify the areas that need to be addressed the most. Christopher completed his undergraduate study in psychology and postgraduate study in Industrial-Organizational Psychology and Teacher Education. He was a teaching fellow with the Teach/Here Teacher Residency Program, now Project Inspire, successfully completed an Internship in Teaching and participated in the 2010-11 Teacher Performance Assessment National Pilot (developed by Stanford University). He has also served as a Clinical Instructor with Project Inspire. Chris has seen firsthand the obstacles facing the students, teachers, and families in impoverished communities.

Contact Chris

- Book Chris to Speak at Your Event - www.morrisseymodel.com or https://www.morrisseymodel.com/book-online

- Schedule a free call to set up the Morrissey Model Program for my school. - https://www.morrisseymodel.com/book-online

- Follow us on Facebook: facebook.com/morrisseymodel

www.ingramcontent.com/pod-product-compliance
Lightning Source LLC
Chambersburg PA
CBHW070458100426
42743CB00010B/1673